REALEMON
BRAND®

easy Cooking with Zing

Meredith® Books
Des Moines, Iowa

This seal assures you that every recipe in *Easy Cooking with Zing* has been tested in the Better Homes and Gardens® Test Kitchen. This means that each recipe is practical and reliable and meets high standards of taste appeal.

Printing Number and Year: 5 4 3 2 1   04 03 02 01 00
ISBN: 0-696-21113-0
Canadian BN: 12348 2887 RT
ReaLemon, ReaLime and Eagle Brand are registered trademarks of Eagle Family Foods, Inc.
Produced by Meredith® Books and Meredith Integrated Marketing, 1716 Locust Street, Des Moines, IA 50309-3023.
Better Homes and Gardens® Test Kitchen Seal is a registered trademark of Meredith Corporation.

a bold new *Taste* revolution is taking hold!

From trendy bistros to backyard barbecues, today's best cooking comes with an exciting focus on freshness. Few ingredients add a burst of fresh flavor to foods as easily and conveniently as ReaLemon® and ReaLime® Juices from Concentrate.

Inside these pages, you'll find inspiring ways to use ReaLemon to bring your cooking to new heights of citrus-sparked appeal. Taste for yourself how ReaLemon adds zing—yet lets the natural flavors of other foods come through. Better yet, cooking with ReaLemon is as simple as home cooking gets, because ReaLemon is virtually foolproof—a zesty flavor enhancer that's never out of season and always consistent in strength and quality, ensuring great results time after time.

Whether you're in the mood for a cookout, a special dinner with family or friends, a quick-to-fix weeknight supper—or just ready to relax over a tall, cool drink on the porch—you'll discover how ReaLemon adds a flavor kick to all your foods.

Pictured on the cover: *Citrus Chicken (recipe, page 9) and Fruit Salsa (recipe, page 32)*

Table of Contents

Credits

Produced by:
Meredith® Books and
Meredith Integrated Marketing,
1716 Locust Street,
Des Moines, IA 50309-3023.

Meredith® Books
Editor: Chuck Smothermon
Design Production:
Craig Hanken
Proofreader: Susan J. Kling
Production Director:
Douglas M. Johnston

Editor in Chief: James D. Blume
Design Director: Matt Strelecki
Managing Editor:
Gregory H. Kayko

Director, Sales & Marketing,
Retail: Michael A. Peterson
Director, Sales & Marketing,
Special Markets: Rita McMullen
Director, Operations:
George A. Susral

Vice President,
General Manager:
Jamie L. Martin

fresh *flavors* anytime

From stir-fries to grill-outs, today's focus is on fresh, simple cooking that lets the natural flavors of foods come through. Cooks everywhere are calling on the flavorful punches of lemon and lime to bring exhilarating results to these contemporary creations, such as Thai Chicken Appetizer Skewers (photo, right; recipe, page 28). Adding ease (and sure-fire results) to this

new age of fresh-focused cooking are ReaLemon® and ReaLime® Juices from Concentrate. Here's our story— and a few tips on how to use these no-fail ingredients to bring zesty results to your meals.

ReaLemon Means True Lemon Flavor

When you're looking for the true, unmistakable taste of lemon, ReaLemon is a natural! That's because it starts with the juice of high-quality lemons, concentrated to a uniform strength. Then, enough filtered water is added to return this concentrate to the natural strength of fresh lemons. A little oil from the peel is added, and the true taste of lemon comes through, time after time. ReaLime is made with the same tried-and-true process, using top-quality limes.

Why ReaLemon?

Fresh lemons can differ in size, juiciness and strength. Since 1934, when ReaLemon was first introduced, cooks have relied on ReaLemon's consistency in strength and quality. Never too weak, never too tart, ReaLemon gives cooks a perfectly balanced ingredient they can rely on to add just the right spark, recipe after recipe. And, while fresh lemons are perishable, ReaLemon has a long shelf life and is easier to keep on hand. It's also more economical than lemons. Furthermore, lemons take time to squeeze and strain. ReaLemon fits into today's fast-paced lifestyle by being easy to use without putting the squeeze on your schedule!

Tips on Using ReaLemon

This book is chock-full of tasty ideas that call on the brisk, lively flavor of ReaLemon to spark meals. But don't stop there! Use ReaLemon in your favorite recipes that call for lemons. Just remember these tips:

■ For recipes that call for the juice of one lemon or one lime, use about 2 to 3 tablespoons of ReaLemon or ReaLime.

■ ReaLemon and ReaLime are easy to keep on hand. Store the unopened bottle in the cupboard. Once it's open, keep the product in the refrigerator until the expiration date.

■ Shake ReaLemon and ReaLime before each use.

■ The 15-ounce ReaLemon plastic squeeze bottle is designed for convenience. The spout makes it easy to add the right amount.

■ The small plastic lemons and limes, often found in the produce section, are available in 2½- and 4½-ounce sizes. These squeezable little gems are easy to tote to picnics and other gatherings.

ReaLemon Family of Products

ReaLemon and ReaLime come in a size and shape for every use.

■ Looking for a good value? Opt for the 32-ounce bottle of ReaLemon so you can call on its great flavor again and again.

■ The 8-ounce ReaLemon and ReaLime bottles are perfect to keep on hand to add zing anytime.

grill
out
Tonight

Sweet and Tangy
Grilled Flank Steak
(recipe, page 12)

Zesty Summer
Squash and Pasta
(recipe, page 70)

Marinate in the morning,
sizzle up some fun tonight!
That's the idea behind many of the
easy recipes in this chapter. All get a
lively flavor punch from ReaLemon® or
ReaLime® to ensure tempting results
you'll look forward to all day.

spicy grilled chicken

The cinnamon, ginger and nutmeg flavors of the pumpkin pie spice add allure to this delightfully exotic dish.

Prep time: 15 minutes   **Marinate time:** 4 to 24 hours
Grill time: 35 to 45 minutes   **Makes:** 4 servings

2 pounds meaty chicken pieces (breasts, thighs and drumsticks)
½ cup ReaLemon® Lemon Juice from Concentrate
¼ cup olive oil
2 cloves garlic, finely chopped
1½ teaspoons pumpkin pie spice (*or* 1 teaspoon ground cinnamon and ½ teaspoon ground allspice)
½ teaspoon salt
½ teaspoon crushed red pepper

Skin and rinse chicken; pat dry. Place chicken in plastic bag set in shallow dish.

For marinade, combine ReaLemon, oil, garlic, spice, salt and red pepper in small bowl. Pour over chicken; seal bag. Marinate in refrigerator 4 to 24 hours, turning occasionally. Drain chicken, reserving marinade.

Grill chicken, bone side up, on rack of uncovered grill directly over *medium* coals 25 minutes, brushing occasionally with marinade. Turn; brush with marinade. Grill 10 to 20 minutes longer or until chicken is tender and no longer pink.

Or, broil, bone side up, on unheated rack of broiler pan 5 to 6 inches from heat 20 minutes, brushing occasionally with marinade. Turn; brush with marinade. Broil 10 to 15 minutes longer.

Discard any remaining marinade.

Nutrition facts per serving: 235 cal., 12 g total fat (3 g sat. fat), 92 mg chol., 174 mg sodium, 1 g carbo., 0 g fiber, 30 g pro.

*G*rilling Hint

To help keep meat, poultry and fish moist during grilling, brush them several times with ReaLemon. And there's a bonus: ReaLemon adds zesty flavor without adding sodium.

citrus chicken

ReaLemon, ReaLime, orange—talk about zing! This simple grilling recipe infuses chicken breasts with a triple hit of citrus sensations (pictured on the cover).

Prep time: 10 minutes   **Marinate time:** 4 to 24 hours
Grill time: 12 to 15 minutes   **Makes:** 4 servings

4   **medium skinless, boneless chicken breast halves (1 pound)**
¼   **cup ReaLemon® Lemon Juice from Concentrate**
2   **tablespoons ReaLime® Lime Juice from Concentrate**
2   **tablespoons orange juice**
1   **tablespoon cooking oil**
1   **teaspoon sugar**
½   **teaspoon dried oregano, crushed**

Rinse chicken; pat dry. Sprinkle with *salt* and *pepper*. Place chicken in plastic bag set in shallow dish.

For marinade, combine ReaLemon, ReaLime, orange juice, oil, sugar and oregano in small bowl. Pour over chicken; seal bag. Marinate in refrigerator 4 to 24 hours, turning occasionally. Drain chicken, reserving marinade.

Grill chicken on rack of uncovered grill directly over *medium* coals 12 to 15 minutes or until tender and no longer pink, turning once and brushing occasionally with marinade during first half of cooking.

Or, broil on unheated rack of broiler pan 4 to 5 inches from heat 12 to 15 minutes, turning once and brushing occasionally with marinade during first half of cooking.

Discard any remaining marinade.

Nutrition facts per serving: 149 cal., 5 g total fat (1 g sat. fat), 59 mg chol., 57 mg sodium, 2 g carbo., 0 g fiber, 22 g pro.

mustard-lemon chicken

A little sweet, a little tart—mustard and lemon are a winning combination.

Prep time: 10 minutes **Marinate time:** 2 to 4 hours
Grill time: 12 to 15 minutes **Makes:** 6 servings

6 **medium skinless, boneless chicken breast halves (1½ pounds)**
⅓ **cup ReaLemon® Lemon Juice from Concentrate**
¼ **cup coarse-grain brown mustard**
3 **tablespoons sugar**
2 **tablespoons cooking oil**

Rinse chicken; pat dry. Place in plastic bag set in shallow dish.

For marinade, combine ReaLemon, mustard, sugar and oil in small bowl. Pour over chicken; seal bag. Marinate in refrigerator 2 to 4 hours, turning occasionally. Drain chicken, reserving marinade.

Grill chicken on rack of uncovered grill directly over *medium* coals 12 to 15 minutes or until tender and no longer pink, turning once and brushing occasionally with some marinade during first half of cooking.

Or, broil on unheated rack of broiler pan 4 to 5 inches from heat 12 to 15 minutes, turning once and brushing occasionally with some marinade during first half of cooking.

Bring remaining marinade to a boil; cover and boil 1 minute. Serve over chicken.

Nutrition facts per serving: 197 cal., 8 g total fat (2 g sat. fat), 59 mg chol., 191 mg sodium, 8 g carbo., 0 g fiber, 22 g pro.

Ready-to-Go Chicken

Enjoy the convenience of marinated chicken breasts anytime. Just place the chicken in a freezer bag, add one of the zesty marinades on page 23 and freeze. When you're caught without anything planned for dinner, simply thaw in the microwave—it's already flavored and ready to cook!

sweet and tangy grilled flank steak

ReaLime and pineapple juice transform your favorite steak sauce into a lively marinade you'll want to savor again and again this summer (photo, pages 6–7).

Prep time: 10 minutes   **Marinate time:** 4 to 24 hours
Grill time: 12 to 14 minutes   **Makes:** 4 to 6 servings

1	**(1- to 1½-pound) beef flank steak**
¾	**cup unsweetened pineapple juice**
⅓	**cup ReaLime® Lime Juice from Concentrate**
¼	**cup steak sauce**

Score meat by making shallow diagonal cuts on one side at 1-inch intervals in diamond pattern. Repeat on other side. Sprinkle with *salt* and *pepper*. Place meat in plastic bag set in shallow dish.

For marinade, combine pineapple juice, ReaLime and steak sauce in small bowl. Pour over meat; seal bag. Marinate in refrigerator 4 to 24 hours, turning occasionally. Drain meat, discarding marinade.

Grill meat on rack of uncovered grill directly over *medium* coals until desired doneness, turning once (allow 12 to 14 minutes for medium). Garnish with fresh herbs, pineapple and tomatoes if desired. To serve, thinly slice meat across grain.

Nutrition facts per serving: 171 cal., 8 g total fat (3 g sat. fat), 53 mg chol., 133 mg sodium, 1 g carbo., 0 g fiber, 22 g pro.

grilled oriental steak

Steak has long ranked among America's favorite grilled foods. Add an Asian update plus a spark of ReaLemon, and a delicious new classic is born.

Prep time: 10 minutes   **Marinate time:** 4 to 24 hours
Grill time: 16 to 18 minutes   **Makes:** 6 to 8 servings

1	**(1½- to 2-pound) boneless beef top sirloin steak, cut 1½ inches thick**
⅓	**cup ReaLemon® Lemon Juice from Concentrate**
¼	**cup soy sauce**
2	**tablespoons cooking oil**
1	**tablespoon sugar**
1	**teaspoon ground ginger**
⅛	**teaspoon garlic powder**

Place meat in plastic bag set in shallow dish. For marinade, combine ReaLemon, soy sauce, oil, sugar, ginger and garlic powder in small bowl. Pour over meat; seal bag. Marinate in refrigerator 4 to 24 hours, turning occasionally. Drain meat, reserving marinade.

Grill meat on rack of uncovered grill directly over *medium* coals until desired doneness, turning once and brushing occasionally with marinade during first half of cooking (allow 16 to 18 minutes for medium rare; 20 to 22 minutes for medium).

Discard any remaining marinade.

Nutrition facts per serving: 231 cal., 12 g total fat (4 g sat. fat), 76 mg chol., 364 mg sodium, 2 g carbo., 0 g fiber, 26 g pro.

tangy lemon-basil burgers

Think there's no improving on the backyard burger? Think again—this creative recipe takes the juicy summer favorite to new heights of flavors, thanks to basil and ReaLemon.

Prep time: 10 minutes   **Grill time:** 14 to 18 minutes   **Makes:** 6 servings

1	**egg**
⅓	**cup unflavored fine dry bread crumbs**
¼	**cup finely chopped onion**
¼	**cup ReaLemon® Lemon Juice from Concentrate**
2	**tablespoons grated Parmesan cheese**
1	**tablespoon chopped fresh basil *or* 1 teaspoon dried basil, crushed**
1½	**pounds lean ground beef**
6	**hamburger buns, split and toasted**
6	**lettuce leaves**

Beat egg, bread crumbs, onion, ReaLemon, Parmesan cheese and basil in medium-sized bowl with fork. Add ground beef; mix well. Shape into six ¾-inch patties.

Grill burgers on rack of uncovered grill directly over *medium* coals 14 to 18 minutes or until no longer pink, turning once.

Or, broil on unheated rack of broiler pan 3 to 4 inches from heat 12 to 14 minutes, turning once.

Serve on buns with lettuce.

Nutrition facts per serving: 397 cal., 19 g total fat (7 g sat. fat), 107 mg chol., 408 mg sodium, 28 g carbo., 0 g fiber, 27 g pro.

italian lemon burgers

Substitute *seasoned fine dry bread crumbs* for unflavored crumbs and 1 teaspoon crushed dried *Italian seasoning* for basil. Proceed as directed. To serve, add 6 thin slices *mozzarella cheese* with lettuce.

Nutrition facts per serving: 403 cal., 18 g total fat (7 g sat. fat), 119 mg chol., 551 mg sodium, 28 g carbo., 1 g fiber, 31 g pro.

*G*rilling Plus!

Take advantage of your hot grill by toasting the buns for this tasty sandwich. Simply place the buns, cut sides down, on the grill rack directly over the coals and grill about 1 minute or until lightly toasted.

Sweet and Sour Ribs

rosemary lamb chops

Enjoy succulent grilled lamb, accented with the wonderful, bold flavor of rosemary and the fresh, tangy taste of ReaLemon.

Prep time: 10 minutes

Marinate time: 4 to 24 hours

Grill time: 10 to 14 minutes

Makes: 4 servings

8 **lamb rib *or* loin chops, cut 1 inch thick**

¼ **cup ReaLemon® Lemon Juice from Concentrate**

¼ **cup balsamic vinegar**

¼ **cup cooking oil**

3 **tablespoons Dijon mustard**

2 **tablespoons chopped fresh rosemary *or* 1 teaspoon dried rosemary, crushed**

2 **cloves garlic, finely chopped**

Trim fat from chops. Sprinkle with *salt* and *pepper*. Place chops in plastic bag set in shallow dish.

For marinade, combine ReaLemon, vinegar, oil, mustard, rosemary and garlic in small bowl. Pour over chops; seal bag. Marinate in refrigerator 4 to 24 hours, turning occasionally. Drain chops, discarding marinade.

Grill chops on rack of uncovered grill directly over *medium* coals until desired doneness, turning once (allow 10 to 14 minutes for medium rare; 14 to 16 minutes for medium).

Nutrition facts per serving: 319 cal., 17 g total fat (6 g sat. fat), 116 mg chol., 253 mg sodium, 3 g carbo., 0 g fiber, 36 g pro.

sweet and sour ribs

Teriyaki sauce, honey and ReaLime impart just the right balance of sweet to sour in this beautifully glazed classic.

Prep time: 10 minutes   **Grill time:** 1¼ to 1½ hours   **Makes:** 4 servings

½ **cup catsup**

⅓ **cup teriyaki sauce**

¼ **cup ReaLime® Lime Juice from Concentrate**

¼ **cup honey**

⅛ **teaspoon garlic powder**

4 **pounds pork loin back ribs *or* meaty pork spareribs**

For sauce, combine catsup, teriyaki sauce, ReaLime, honey and garlic powder in small bowl. Cut ribs into serving-size pieces. Brush with some of the sauce.

Arrange *medium-hot* coals around drip pan in grill with cover. Place ribs on grill rack over pan. Cover and grill 1¼ to

1½ hours or until tender and no longer pink, brushing occasionally with sauce during last 30 minutes.

Or, preheat oven to 350°. Place ribs, bone side up, in shallow roasting pan. Bake 1 hour. Drain fat. Turn ribs; brush with some of the sauce. Cover and bake 45 to 60 minutes longer.

Bring remaining sauce to a boil; cover and boil 1 minute. Serve over ribs.

Nutrition facts per serving: 885 cal., 57 g total fat (22 g sat. fat), 177 mg chol., 1,529 mg sodium, 31 g carbo., 1 g fiber, 60 g pro.

plum-sauced pork chops

Smoky and sweet—who'd guess that something this intriguing takes so few ingredients and so little effort?

Prep time: 20 minutes   **Grill time:** 25 to 30 minutes   **Makes:** 4 servings

¾ **cup plum *or* apricot preserves**
¼ **cup ReaLemon® Lemon Juice from Concentrate**
2 **teaspoons soy sauce**
½ **teaspoon dried sage, crushed**
2 **tablespoons sliced green onion *or* scallion**
4 **pork loin *or* rib chops, cut 1¼ inches thick**

For sauce, combine plum or apricot preserves, ReaLemon, soy sauce and sage in small saucepan. Cook and stir over low heat until preserves are melted. Stir in green onion or scallion. Trim fat from chops.

Grill chops on rack of uncovered grill directly over *medium* coals 25 to 30 minutes or until no longer pink and juices run clear, turning once and brushing with some sauce during last 10 minutes.

Or, broil on unheated rack of broiler pan 3 to 4 inches from heat 18 to 22 minutes, turning once and brushing with some sauce during last 10 minutes.

Bring remaining sauce to a boil; cover and boil 1 minute. Serve over chops.

Nutrition facts per serving: 349 cal., 10 g total fat (3 g sat. fat), 68 mg chol., 234 mg sodium, 43 g carbo., 1 g fiber, 22 g pro.

Controlling Flare-Ups

Meat juices dripping onto hot coals may cause sudden flare-ups that can make your meat taste charred. To reduce flare-ups, raise the grill rack, space the hot coals farther apart or remove a few coals. As a last resort, remove the food and mist the fire with water. Once the flames die down, start grilling again.

lime-marinated pork chops

Bring some tropical-island fun to your backyard with this spicy little number. Round out the meal with Wild Rice Salad (recipe, page 66) and fresh fruit.

Prep time: 10 minutes **Marinate time:** 4 to 24 hours
Grill time: 8 to 11 minutes **Makes:** 4 servings

4 **boneless pork loin chops,**
  cut ¾ inch thick
¼ **teaspoon salt**
¾ **cup ReaLime® Lime Juice**
  from Concentrate
1 **medium onion, chopped**
1 **clove garlic, finely chopped**
½ **teaspoon ground cumin**
½ **teaspoon crushed red pepper**

Trim fat from chops. Sprinkle with salt. Place pork chops in plastic bag set in shallow dish.

For marinade, combine ReaLime, onion, garlic, cumin and red pepper in small bowl. Pour over chops; seal bag. Marinate in refrigerator 4 to 24 hours, turning occasionally. Remove chops, discarding marinade.

Grill chops on rack of uncovered grill directly over *medium* coals 8 to 11 minutes or until no longer pink and juices run clear, turning once.

Or, broil on unheated rack of broiler pan 3 to 4 inches from heat 6 to 8 minutes, turning once.

Nutrition facts per serving: 185 cal., 9 g total fat (3 g sat. fat), 64 mg chol., 191 mg sodium, 4 g carbo., 0 g fiber, 20 g pro.

lemon-thyme fish fillets

Quick-cooking fish on the grill is really catching on, and it fits perfectly into health-conscious, time-crunched lifestyles. This herb-ReaLemon marinade makes a delicious way to tap into the trend.

Prep time: 10 minutes   **Marinate time:** 30 minutes
Grill time: 4 to 6 minutes   **Makes:** 4 servings

1 **pound fresh *or* thawed frozen skinless cod, orange roughy *or* catfish fillets, ½ inch thick**
⅓ **cup ReaLemon® Lemon Juice from Concentrate**
1 **tablespoon chopped fresh thyme *or* 1 teaspoon dried thyme, crushed**
1 **tablespoon olive oil**
½ **teaspoon garlic salt**
⅛ **teaspoon pepper**

Rinse fish; pat dry. Cut into 4 serving-size pieces if necessary. Place fish in shallow dish.

For marinade, combine ReaLemon, thyme, oil, garlic salt and pepper in small bowl. Pour over fish. Marinate at room temperature 30 minutes or in refrigerator 1 to 2 hours. Drain fish, discarding marinade.

Place fish in well-greased grill basket. Tuck under any thin edges. Grill fish on rack of uncovered grill directly over *medium* coals 4 to 6 minutes or until fish flakes easily when tested with a fork, turning once.

Or, broil on greased unheated rack of broiler pan, tucking under any thin edges, 4 inches from heat 4 to 6 minutes.

Nutrition facts per serving: 91 cal., 1 g total fat (0 g sat. fat), 45 mg chol., 97 mg sodium, 0 g carbo., 0 g fiber, 19 g pro.

Delicate Fish

Fish is a great candidate for cooking on the grill, but it needs a little extra care to prevent it from breaking apart. Placing fish fillets in a wire grill basket helps. Spray the basket with no-stick cooking spray or brush with oil before adding the fish.

lemon-dill shrimp kabobs

Infuse shrimp and vegetables with a ReaLemon-dill marinade for a dish bursting with the tastes of summer.

Prep time: 30 minutes   **Marinate time:** 30 minutes
Grill time: 10 to 12 minutes   **Makes:** 4 servings

- 1 **pound fresh *or* thawed frozen large shrimp in shells**
- ¼ **cup ReaLemon® Lemon Juice from Concentrate**
- 1 **tablespoon chopped fresh dill *or* 1 teaspoon dried dillweed**
- 1 **tablespoon olive oil**
- 1 **clove garlic, finely chopped**
- ¼ **teaspoon salt**
- ⅛ **teaspoon black pepper**
- 1 **medium zucchini, sliced ½ inch thick**
- 1 **cup red *and/or* yellow bell pepper cut into 1-inch pieces**

Peel, devein and rinse shrimp. Place shrimp in medium-sized deep bowl.

For marinade, combine ReaLemon, chopped dill, oil, garlic, salt and black pepper in small bowl. Pour over shrimp. Marinate at room temperature 30 minutes or in refrigerator 1 to 2 hours.

Meanwhile, cook zucchini in small amount of boiling water in small covered saucepan 2 minutes. Drain.

Drain shrimp, reserving marinade. Thread shrimp, zucchini and bell pepper on 8 metal skewers.

Grill kabobs on rack of uncovered grill directly over *medium* coals 10 to 12 minutes or until shrimp turn pink and vegetables are tender, turning once and brushing occasionally with some marinade during first half of cooking.

Or, broil on unheated rack of broiler pan 3 to 4 inches from heat 10 to 12 minutes, turning once and brushing occasionally with some marinade during first half of cooking.

Discard any remaining marinade. Garnish with fresh dill sprigs if desired.

Nutrition facts per serving: 110 cal., 4 g total fat (1 g sat. fat), 131 mg chol., 287 mg sodium, 4 g carbo., 1 g fiber, 14 g pro. Daily values: 19% vit. A, 42% vit. C.

Skewer Substitute

No metal skewers? Use bamboo ones instead. Just be sure to soak the skewers in water for at least 30 minutes before grilling so they do not burn.

marinated salmon fillets

This zippy marinade—made extra easy by calling on your favorite Italian salad dressing—works wonders with haddock or orange roughy as well as with salmon.

Prep time: 10 minutes **Marinate time:** 30 minutes
Grill time: 8 to 12 minutes **Makes:** 6 servings

1½ **pounds fresh *or* thawed frozen skinless salmon, haddock *or* orange roughy fillets, 1 inch thick**
⅓ **cup bottled Italian salad dressing**
¼ **cup ReaLemon® Lemon Juice from Concentrate**
3 **tablespoons honey**

Rinse fish; pat dry. Cut into 6 serving-size pieces if necessary. Place fish in shallow dish.

For marinade, combine salad dressing, ReaLemon and honey in small bowl. Pour over fish. Marinate at room temperature 30 minutes or in refrigerator 1 to 2 hours. Drain fish, reserving marinade.

Place fish in well-greased grill basket. Tuck under any thin edges. Grill fish on rack of uncovered grill directly over *medium* coals 8 to 12 minutes or until fish flakes easily when tested with a fork, turning once and brushing occasionally with marinade during first half of cooking.

Or, broil on greased unheated rack of broiler pan, tucking under any thin edges, 4 inches from heat 8 to 12 minutes, turning once and brushing occasionally with marinade during first half of cooking.

Discard any remaining marinade.

Nutrition facts per serving: 138 cal., 6 g total fat (1 g sat. fat), 20 mg chol., 108 mg sodium, 4 g carbo., 0 g fiber, 16 g pro.

*S*leight of Hand

When marinades, sauces and salad dressings call for up to 3 tablespoons of wine or vinegar, make the switch to ReaLemon for great zesty flavor.

create-a-lemon marinade

ReaLemon works miracles in marinades. Not only does its flavor add zip and freshness, but it also helps tenderize the meat.

Prep time: 5 minutes   **Makes:** 4 servings

½ **cup ReaLemon® Lemon Juice from Concentrate**
⅓ **cup cooking oil *or* olive oil**
1 **clove garlic, finely chopped**
¼ **teaspoon salt**
⅛ **teaspoon pepper**

For marinade, combine ReaLemon, oil, garlic, salt and pepper in small bowl.

Use to marinate 1 pound boneless or 1½ pounds bone-in poultry, beef, pork or lamb in refrigerator 4 to 24 hours, or fish or seafood at room temperature 30 minutes or in refrigerator 1 to 2 hours.

Drain and use marinade to brush on meat during first half of grilling. Discard any remaining marinade.

Nutrition facts per serving with chicken: 182 cal., 13 g total fat (2 g sat. fat), 46 mg chol., 109 mg sodium, 1 g carbo., 0 g fiber, 15 g pro.

curry marinade

Add ¼ cup chopped *mango chutney* and 2 teaspoons *curry powder.* Proceed as directed, using beef, pork, lamb or poultry.

Nutrition facts per serving with beef: 306 cal., 19 g total fat (5 g sat. fat), 76 mg chol., 128 mg sodium, 6 g carbo., 0 g fiber, 26 g pro.

oriental marinade

Add 3 tablespoons *hoisin sauce* and 1 tablespoon *soy sauce.* Proceed as directed, using pork, beef for kabobs or poultry.

Nutrition facts per serving with pork: 237 cal., 16 g total fat (4 g sat. fat), 51 mg chol., 356 mg sodium, 5 g carbo., 0 g fiber, 16 g pro.

herb marinade

Add 1 tablespoon chopped fresh *parsley;* 1 tablespoon chopped fresh *basil* or 1 teaspoon dried *basil,* crushed; 1 tablespoon *honey* and 1 teaspoon chopped fresh *oregano* or ¼ teaspoon dried *oregano,* crushed. Proceed as directed, using fish, seafood or poultry.

Nutrition facts per serving with fish: 196 cal., 10 g total fat (2 g sat. fat), 60 mg chol., 163 mg sodium, 3 g carbo., 0 g fiber, 21 g pro.

southwestern marinade

Add ¼ cup *salsa,* 1 tablespoon chopped fresh *cilantro* and 1 to 2 teaspoons *chili powder.* Proceed as directed, using poultry, pork or beef.

Nutrition facts per serving with chicken: 197 cal., 14 g total fat (3 g sat. fat), 51 mg chol., 150 mg sodium, 2 g carbo., 0 g fiber, 17 g pro.

beef, pork and lamb grilling chart

Place the meat on the rack of an uncovered grill directly over preheated coals. Grill for the time given below or until done, turning meat over halfway through grilling time.

Cut	Thickness	Coal Temperature	Doneness	Grilling Time
BEEF				
Flank steak	¾ to 1 inch	Medium	Medium	12 to 14 minutes
Ground meat patties	¾ inch (4 per pound)	Medium	No longer pink	14 to 18 minutes
Steak (blade, chuck, top round)	1 inch 1½ inches	Medium Medium	Medium rare Medium Medium rare Medium	14 to 16 minutes 18 to 20 minutes 19 to 26 minutes 27 to 32 minutes
Steak (porterhouse, rib, rib eye, sirloin, T-bone, tenderloin, top loin)	1 inch 1¼ to 1½ inches	Medium Medium	Medium rare Medium Medium rare Medium	8 to 12 minutes 12 to 15 minutes 14 to 18 minutes 18 to 22 minutes
PORK				
Chop	¾ inch 1¼ to 1½ inches	Medium Medium	No longer pink; juices run clear No longer pink; juices run clear	8 to 11 minutes 25 to 30 minutes
LAMB				
Chop	1 inch	Medium	Medium rare Medium	10 to 14 minutes 14 to 16 minutes
KABOBS	1-inch cubes	Medium	Medium	12 to 14 minutes

poultry, fish and seafood grilling charts

POULTRY

Place the poultry, bone side up, on the rack of an uncovered grill directly over preheated coals. Grill for the time given below or until done. (Note: White meat will cook slightly faster.) Turn the poultry over halfway through grilling time.

Type of Poultry	Weight	Coal Temperature	Doneness	Grilling Time
Chicken breast half (skinless and boneless)	4 to 5 ounces each	Medium	Tender; no longer pink	12 to 15 minutes
Chicken pieces (meaty)	2 to 2½ pounds total	Medium	Tender; no longer pink	35 to 45 minutes
Turkey breast tenderloin steak	4 to 6 ounces each	Medium	Tender; no longer pink	12 to 15 minutes

FISH AND SEAFOOD

Place fish fillets in a well-greased grill basket. For fish steaks and whole fish, grease the grill rack. Place the fish or seafood on the rack of an uncovered grill directly over preheated coals. Grill for the time given below or until done. Turn the fish over halfway through grilling time.

Form of Fish	Weight, Size or Thickness	Coal Temperature	Doneness	Grilling Time
Whole fish (cleaned)	½ to 1½ pounds	Medium	Flakes	7 to 9 minutes per ½ pound
Fillets, steaks, cubes (for kabobs)	½ to 1 inch thick	Medium	Flakes	4 to 6 minutes per ½-inch thickness
Sea scallops (for kabobs)	(12 to 15 per pound)	Medium	Opaque	5 to 8 minutes
Shrimp (for kabobs)	Medium (20 per pound)	Medium	Turns pink	6 to 8 minutes

Romaine and Toasted
Walnut Salad (recipe,
page 62)

flavorful
celebrations

Looking for something special—without the hassle? Most of these sophisticated recipes boast prep times of 15 minutes or less. The secret? ReaLemon and ReaLime add dazzle—on the double— making these creations exciting and easy.

Beef Tenderloin with Honey-Peach Sauce (recipe, page 36)

thai chicken appetizer skewers

Sweet, nutty, spicy and citrus-fresh—this great recipe lets you treat your guests to a spectrum of Thai flavors (photo, page 4).

Prep time: 20 minutes   **Grill time:** 8 to 10 minutes
Makes: 12 servings

¼ **cup ReaLime® Lime Juice from Concentrate**
¼ **cup bottled Italian salad dressing**
1 **tablespoon reduced-sodium soy sauce**
1 **pound skinless, boneless chicken breast halves**
⅓ **cup purchased unsweetened coconut milk**
¼ **cup creamy peanut butter**
3 **tablespoons ReaLime® Lime Juice from Concentrate**
2 **tablespoons reduced-sodium chicken broth**
2 **cloves garlic, finely chopped**
⅛ **to ¼ teaspoon ground red pepper**

Combine ¼ cup ReaLime, salad dressing and soy sauce in small bowl. Set aside.

Rinse chicken; pat dry. Slice chicken across grain into 3-inch-long strips ¼ to ⅜ inch thick. Thread chicken, accordion-style, onto twelve 6-inch metal skewers. Set aside.

For sauce, combine coconut milk, peanut butter, 3 tablespoons ReaLime, broth, garlic and red pepper in small saucepan. Cook and stir over medium heat until slightly thickened, smooth and bubbly. Keep warm.

Grill kabobs on rack of uncovered grill directly over *medium* coals 8 to 10 minutes or until chicken is tender and no longer pink, turning once and brushing often with soy mixture during last 5 minutes of cooking.

Or, broil on unheated rack of broiler pan 4 to 5 inches from heat 8 to 10 minutes, turning once and brushing often with soy mixture during last 5 minutes of cooking.

Serve sauce with kabobs. Garnish with crushed red pepper if desired.

Nutrition facts per serving: 111 cal., 7 g total fat (2 g sat. fat), 20 mg chol., 138 mg sodium, 3 g carbo., 0 g fiber, 9 g pro.

Stylish but Easy!

When it comes to garnishing food, follow this golden rule: Keep it simple. Dress up main dishes with a simple sprig of fresh herb and desserts with a dusting of unsweetened cocoa powder. For added flair, accent salads with a ruffled leaf of kale or leaf lettuce. Add interest to foods by cutting them into eye-catching shapes. For example, bias-slice carrots or shred fresh spinach.

lemon-glazed appetizer meatballs

Appetizer meatballs go uptown with a tasty sweet-and-sour glaze that makes them shine like gems and taste equally precious.

Prep time: 10 minutes   **Cook time:** 15 minutes
Makes: 16 servings

1   **cup (12-ounce jar) red currant *or* grape jelly**
⅓   **cup ReaLemon® Lemon Juice from Concentrate**
⅓   **cup barbecue sauce**
1   **tablespoon soy sauce**
¼   **teaspoon pepper**
1   **(16-ounce) package frozen cooked meatballs**
1   **(15¼-ounce) can pineapple chunks packed with juice, well drained**

Combine red currant or grape jelly, ReaLemon, barbecue sauce, soy sauce and pepper in large saucepan. Cook and stir over medium heat until bubbly. Stir in meatballs.

Boil gently 15 minutes or until meatballs are heated through and sauce is slightly thickened, stirring occasionally. Stir in pineapple; heat through.

Nutrition facts per serving: 160 cal., 7 g total fat (3 g sat. fat), 18 mg chol., 352 mg sodium, 21 g carbo., 1 g fiber, 5 g pro.

creamy bean dip

Even if you're watching what you eat, you can still dip into this dip. It's low in fat compared to most.

Prep time: 10 minutes   **Makes:** 8 servings

1   **(15-ounce) can garbanzo beans (chickpeas) *or* great northern beans, rinsed and drained**
¼   **cup ReaLemon® Lemon Juice from Concentrate**
¼   **cup creamy peanut butter**
2   **tablespoons water**
2   **cloves garlic, finely chopped**
   Dash salt
   Thinly sliced green onion with tops
   Fresh vegetable dippers *and/or* bagel chips

Combine garbanzo or great northern beans, ReaLemon, peanut butter, water, garlic and salt in food processor bowl. Cover and process until smooth.

Transfer to serving bowl. Sprinkle with green onion. Serve immediately or chill up to 3 days. Serve with vegetables and/or chips.

Nutrition facts per serving of dip: 92 cal., 5 g total fat (1 g sat. fat), 0 mg chol., 226 mg sodium, 9 g carbo., 3 g fiber, 4 g pro.

lemony avocado dip

The splash of ReaLemon not only adds a flavorful spark, but keeps the avocado from turning brown, too.

Prep time: 10 minutes   **Makes:** 14 servings

3   ripe medium avocados,
      seeded, peeled and cut up
1   (8-ounce) carton dairy
      sour cream
½   small onion, cut up
¼   cup ReaLemon® Lemon Juice
      from Concentrate
3   tablespoons grated
      Parmesan cheese
1   tablespoon chopped fresh
      cilantro *or* parsley
3   cloves garlic, halved
½   teaspoon salt
      Few dashes bottled hot
      pepper sauce

Fresh vegetable dippers
***and/or* tortilla chips**

Combine avocados, sour cream, onion, ReaLemon, Parmesan cheese, cilantro or parsley, garlic, salt and pepper sauce in food processor bowl or blender container. Cover and process until smooth.

Transfer to serving bowl. Serve immediately or chill up to 24 hours. Serve with vegetables and/or chips.

Nutrition facts per serving of dip: 104 cal., 11 g total fat (2 g sat. fat), 8 mg chol., 114 mg sodium, 2 g carbo., 6 g fiber, 2 g pro.

shrimp and mango appetizer

The spectacular flavors of this elegant-yet-easy starter are great with mango or papaya.

Prep time: 15 minutes   **Marinate time: 2** to 4 hours   **Makes:** 8 to 10 servings

1½ **pounds peeled cooked shrimp**
¼ **cup ReaLemon® Lemon Juice from Concentrate**
¼ **cup olive oil**
2 **tablespoons white wine vinegar**
2 **tablespoons chili sauce**
1 **tablespoon honey**
1 **teaspoon grated fresh ginger**
1 **clove garlic, finely chopped**
¼ **teaspoon salt**
   Kale *or* lettuce
1 **medium mango *or* papaya, peeled, seeded and sliced**

Place shrimp in medium-sized deep bowl. For marinade, combine ReaLemon, oil, vinegar, chili sauce, honey, ginger, garlic and salt in screw-top jar. Cover and shake well. Pour over shrimp. Marinate in refrigerator 2 to 4 hours, stirring occasionally.

Drain shrimp, discarding marinade. Transfer shrimp to serving bowl. Arrange kale or lettuce and mango or papaya around shrimp.

Nutrition facts per serving: 130 cal., 4 g total fat (1 g sat. fat), 166 mg chol., 253 mg sodium, 4 g carbo., 0 g fiber, 18 g pro. Daily values: 11% vit. A, 24% vit. C.

artichokes with lemon-butter sauce

The delightful zest of ReaLemon provides a pleasing contrast to the velvety meat of this most elegant of vegetables.

Prep time: 15 minutes   **Cook time:** 20 to 30 minutes   **Makes:** 4 servings

4   artichokes (10 ounces each)
**⅓   cup ReaLemon® Lemon
       Juice from Concentrate**
⅓   cup butter *or* margarine
**1   tablespoon chopped fresh
       basil *or* 1 teaspoon dried
       basil, crushed**
¼   teaspoon garlic powder

Trim artichoke stems and remove loose outer leaves. Cut off 1 inch from each top; snip off sharp leaf tips. Brush cut edges with 2 tablespoons of the ReaLemon.

Bring large amount of lightly salted water and 2 tablespoons of the ReaLemon to a boil in large saucepan. Add artichokes; return to a boil. Reduce heat; cover and simmer 20 to 30 minutes or until leaf pulls out easily. Drain upside down on paper towels.

Meanwhile, for sauce, melt butter or margarine in small saucepan over low heat. Stir in basil, garlic powder and remaining ReaLemon. Serve with artichokes.

Nutrition facts per serving: 270 cal., 16 g total fat (9 g sat. fat), 41 mg chol., 410 mg sodium, 31 g carbo., 14 g fiber, 10 g pro. Daily values: 18% vit. A, 35% vit. C.

fruit salsa

Make this colorful salsa a summertime standby. It's a stunning topper for grilled fish or chicken, great to munch with chips, and it's fat free to boot! [Pictured on the cover with Citrus Chicken (recipe, page 9).]

Prep time: 20 minutes   **Chill time:** 4 to 24 hours   **Makes:** 6 to 8 servings

**4   Italian plum tomatoes,
       chopped**
**1   cup chopped fresh pineapple
       or 2 (8-ounce) cans crushed
       pineapple packed with
       juice, drained**
**½   cup chopped green *and/or*
       red bell pepper**
⅓   cup red onion slivers
**¼   cup ReaLime® Lime Juice
       from Concentrate**
**3   tablespoons chopped fresh
       cilantro**
**1   *or* 2 fresh jalapeño peppers,
       seeded and finely chopped**

Combine tomatoes, pineapple, bell pepper, onion, ReaLime, chopped cilantro and jalapeño pepper(s) in medium-sized bowl. Chill 4 to 24 hours.

Serve using a slotted spoon. Garnish with fresh cilantro sprig if desired.

Nutrition facts per serving: 36 cal., 0 g total fat (0 g sat. fat), 0 mg chol., 8 mg sodium, 9 g carbo., 1 g fiber, 1 g pro. Daily values: 4% vit. A, 60% vit. C.

turkey piccata

There are many versions of the luscious piccata sauce, but all include a distinct kiss of lemon. Impress your guests with this version of the classic served over turkey.

Prep time: 15 minutes   **Cook time:** 6 to 8 minutes   **Makes:** 6 servings

1½   **pounds turkey breast slices (cutlets), cut ½ inch thick**
2   **tablespoons margarine or butter**
3   **cups sliced fresh mushrooms (8 ounces)**
¼   **cup ReaLemon® Lemon Juice from Concentrate**
3   **tablespoons water**
2   **tablespoons chopped fresh basil *or* 2 teaspoons dried basil, crushed**
1   **tablespoon cornstarch**
½   **teaspoon instant chicken bouillon granules**
2   **tablespoons chopped fresh parsley**

Rinse turkey; pat dry. Sprinkle with *salt* and *pepper*. Cook turkey in hot margarine or butter in 12-inch skillet over medium-high heat 2 to 4 minutes or until no longer pink, turning once. Remove; cover and keep warm.

For sauce, add mushrooms to skillet. Cook and stir over medium heat 1 minute. Combine ReaLemon, water, basil, cornstarch and bouillon granules. Add to skillet, scraping up crusty browned bits. Cook and stir until boiling; cook and stir 2 minutes longer. Serve over turkey and sprinkle with parsley.

Nutrition facts per serving: 164 cal., 6 g total fat (1 g sat. fat), 50 mg chol., 169 mg sodium, 4 g carbo., 1 g fiber, 22 g pro.

baked lime chicken

Did you just find out today that you'll be entertaining tonight? Refreshing ReaLime and a few pantry staples make a dynamite marinade for this impromptu entrée.

Prep time: 10 minutes   **Marinate time:** 4 to 24 hours
Bake time: 45 to 55 minutes   **Makes:** 6 servings

6   **medium bone-in chicken breast halves (3 pounds)**
½   **cup ReaLime® Lime Juice from Concentrate**
2   **tablespoons olive oil *or* cooking oil**
1   **tablespoon chopped fresh thyme *or* 1 teaspoon dried thyme, crushed**
½   **teaspoon onion salt**
¼   **teaspoon pepper**

Skin chicken if desired. Rinse chicken; pat dry. Place chicken in plastic bag set in shallow dish. For marinade, combine ReaLime, oil, thyme, onion salt and pepper. Pour over chicken; seal bag. Marinate in refrigerator 4 to 24 hours, turning occasionally.

Preheat oven to 375°. Drain chicken, reserving marinade. Arrange chicken, meaty side down, in 15x10-inch baking pan. Bake 25 minutes. Drain fat. Turn and brush with marinade. Bake 20 to 30 minutes longer or until tender and no longer pink.

Nutrition facts per serving: 226 cal., 11 g total fat (3 g sat. fat), 83 mg chol., 138 mg sodium, 1 g carbo., 0 g fiber, 29 g pro.

tarragon-lemon roast chicken

Give the Sunday roast a fresh new update with this easy entrée. Its sauce is infused with tarragon and ReaLemon. Complete the meal with Lemon Chess Pie (recipe, page 79).

Prep time: 15 minutes
Stand time: 10 minutes

Bake time: 1 to 1¼ hours
Makes: 6 servings

1 (2½- to 3-pound) whole broiler-fryer chicken
⅓ cup ReaLemon® Lemon Juice from Concentrate
1 tablespoon olive oil
¾ teaspoon dried tarragon or 1 teaspoon dried basil, crushed
2 cloves garlic, finely chopped
½ teaspoon salt
¼ teaspoon pepper

Preheat oven to 375°. Rinse chicken; pat dry. Skewer neck skin to back; tie legs to tail. Twist wings under back. Place, breast side up, on rack in shallow roasting pan.

Combine ReaLemon, oil, dried tarragon or basil, garlic, salt and pepper in small bowl. Brush half of the mixture over chicken.

Insert meat thermometer into center of inside thigh muscle if desired (bulb should not touch bone).

Bake chicken 1 to 1¼ hours or until drumsticks move easily, juices run clear and thermometer registers 180° to 185°, brushing occasionally with remaining lemon mixture.

Remove from oven; cover and let stand 10 minutes before carving. Garnish with fresh fruit and tarragon sprigs if desired.

Nutrition facts per serving: 203 cal., 12 g total fat (3 g sat. fat), 66 mg chol., 242 mg sodium, 1 g carbo., 0 g fiber, 21 g pro.

Parties Made Easy

Hosting a party doesn't have to be a lot of work. Use these tips to help simplify your next get-together:

■ **Keep the menu to one style—either all finger foods or all knife-and-fork foods.**

■ **Build your menu around one of the simple, reliable main dishes in this chapter.**

■ **Select precut vegetables and fruits and serve with one of the easy dips in this chapter.**

■ **Rely on a good bakery for high-quality breads and rolls.**

beef tenderloin with honey-peach sauce

Here, the fruity sauce provides a lovely contrast to the rich beef for an entrée that's opulent, yet easy (photo, pages 26–27).

Prep time: 10 minutes
Stand time: 15 minutes

Bake time: 30 to 40 minutes
Makes: 8 to 10 servings

1	**(2- to 2½-pound) beef tenderloin**
1	**cup unsweetened pineapple juice**
⅓	**cup ReaLemon® Lemon Juice from Concentrate**
2	**tablespoons cornstarch**
2	**tablespoons butter *or* margarine**
2	**tablespoons honey**
1	**teaspoon instant beef bouillon granules**
1½	**cups fresh *or* thawed frozen peach slices, chopped**

Preheat oven to 425°. If meat is long and thin, fold narrow ends under and tie. If meat is flat and wide, tie crosswise in 2 or 3 places to make rounder. Place meat on rack in shallow roasting pan. Insert meat thermometer in center. Sprinkle with *salt* and *pepper*.

Bake 30 to 40 minutes or until thermometer registers 140° for medium rare. Remove from pan. Remove strings if tied. Cover and let stand 15 minutes (meat temperature will rise 5° during standing).

Meanwhile, for sauce, combine pineapple juice, ReaLemon and cornstarch in medium-sized saucepan. Add butter or margarine, honey and bouillon granules.

Cook and stir until thickened and bubbly. Cook and stir 2 minutes longer. Stir in peaches; heat through.

Thinly slice meat across grain. Serve with sauce.

Nutrition facts per serving: 238 cal., 10 g total fat (5 g sat. fat), 72 mg chol., 209 mg sodium, 15 g carbo., 1 g fiber, 22 g pro.

*U*sing a Meat Thermometer

A meat thermometer guarantees perfectly cooked meat roasted the way you like it. Insert the thermometer into the center of the thickest portion or largest muscle of the meat. It should not touch any fat or bone or the pan. When the meat reaches the desired doneness, push in the thermometer a little farther. If the temperature drops, continue cooking. If it stays the same, remove the meat from the heat.

herb marinated pork roast

Marinating pork in the ReaLemon-based marinade results in a tender, succulent roast.

Prep time: 10 minutes   **Marinate time:** 6 to 24 hours
Bake time: 1¼ to 1¾ hours   **Stand time:** 15 minutes
Makes: 6 to 8 servings

1   (2- to 3-pound) boneless
    pork top loin roast
    (single loin)
½   cup ReaLemon® Lemon Juice
    from Concentrate
¼   cup reduced-sodium
    soy sauce
1   teaspoon dried oregano,
    crushed
1   teaspoon dried basil, crushed
1   clove garlic, finely chopped
¼   teaspoon pepper

Place meat in plastic bag set in shallow dish. For marinade, combine ReaLemon, soy sauce, oregano, basil, garlic and pepper. Pour over meat; seal bag. Marinate in refrigerator 6 to 24 hours, turning occasionally.

Preheat oven to 325°. Drain meat, discarding marinade. Place meat on rack in shallow roasting pan. Insert meat thermometer into center. Bake 1¼ to 1¾ hours or until thermometer registers 155°. Remove from pan. Cover and let stand 15 minutes (meat temperature will rise 5° during standing).

Nutrition facts per serving: 184 cal., 10 g total fat (3 g sat. fat), 68 mg chol., 146 mg sodium, 1 g carbo., 0 g fiber, 22 g pro.

linguine with lemon and scallops

Enhancing seafood with lemon is an age-old culinary practice, but this colorful, light dish, with its Asian flavors, is a thoroughly contemporary take on the tradition.

Prep time: 10 minutes   **Cook time:** 8 to 10 minutes   **Makes:** 4 servings

8   ounces packaged dried
     linguine
2   cups fresh pea pods,
     trimmed
12   ounces fresh sea scallops
1½   cups packaged shredded
     carrots
½   cup chicken broth
2   tablespoons reduced-sodium
     soy sauce
½   teaspoon grated fresh ginger
¼   to ½ teaspoon crushed
     red pepper
¼   cup ReaLemon® Lemon Juice
     from Concentrate
2½   teaspoons cornstarch

Cook linguine in lightly salted water according to package directions, adding pea pods last 2 minutes. Drain; return to pan. Meanwhile, rinse scallops; pat dry. Halve any large scallops. Set aside.

Combine carrots, broth, soy, ginger and red pepper in medium-sized skillet. Bring to a boil. Combine ReaLemon and cornstarch; add to skillet. Add scallops.

Cook and stir gently until bubbly. Cook and stir gently 2 minutes longer or until scallops turn opaque. Pour over linguine mixture; toss gently to coat.

Nutrition facts per serving: 334 cal., 2 g total fat (0 g sat. fat), 26 mg chol., 524 mg sodium, 57 g carbo., 5 g fiber, 22 g pro. Daily values: 117% vit. A, 29% vit. C.

salmon salad with peppers and olives

It's up to you (and your schedule). You can serve the salmon warm. Or, for a make-ahead entrée, cook the salmon beforehand, chill, then serve atop the crisp, fresh salad.

Prep time: 20 minutes   **Cook time:** 8 to 12 minutes   **Makes:** 4 servings

¼ cup ReaLime® Lime Juice from Concentrate

3 tablespoons olive oil *or* cooking oil

2 tablespoons water

4 teaspoons white wine Worcestershire sauce

1 tablespoon chopped fresh basil *or* 1 teaspoon dried basil, crushed

2 teaspoons sugar

¼ teaspoon salt

⅛ teaspoon black pepper

1 pound fresh *or* thawed frozen skinless salmon, cod *or* orange roughy fillets, 1 inch thick

6 cups prewashed spinach, stemmed and coarsely shredded

2 medium red *and/or* yellow bell peppers, cut into thin bite-size strips

½ cup pitted kalamata olives, chopped

For dressing, combine ReaLime, oil, water, Worcestershire sauce, basil, sugar, salt and black pepper in small bowl. Set aside ½ cup dressing.

Rinse fish; pat dry. Cut into 4 serving-size pieces if necessary. Place fish on greased unheated rack of broiler pan. Tuck under any thin edges. Brush with some of the remaining dressing.

Broil 4 inches from heat 5 minutes. Turn; brush with remaining dressing. Broil 3 to 7 minutes longer or until fish flakes easily when tested with a fork.

Serve fish on top of spinach. Arrange bell peppers around fish; sprinkle with chopped olives. Drizzle with reserved dressing. Garnish with pitted whole kalamata olives if desired.

Nutrition facts per serving: 293 cal., 20 g total fat (3 g sat. fat), 20 mg chol., 868 mg sodium, 11 g carbo., 3 g fiber, 19 g pro. Daily values: 101% vit. A, 142% vit. C.

Boost the Flavor

Add extra zing to poached fish or chicken by pouring a little ReaLemon or ReaLime into the cooking liquid.

weeknight cooking
with a twist

Got the dinnertime doldrums?
Depart from the ho-hum and experience
the zing ReaLemon brings to easy
weeknight meals. The colorful
stir-fries, sparkling seafood, sizzling
fajitas and other speedy suppers
are sure to add a spark
to dinnertime.

Chicken and
Vegetable Stir-Fry
(recipe, page 44)

lemon chicken

Sure, you could pick up take-out food tonight. But with this dish, inspired by a Chinese restaurant favorite, you can make it fresher and better in the time it takes to order out.

Prep time: 15 minutes   **Cook time:** 8 to 10 minutes   **Makes:** 6 servings

6 **medium skinless, boneless chicken breast halves (1½ pounds)**
¼ **cup unsifted flour**
¼ **teaspoon salt**
¼ **teaspoon pepper**
2 **tablespoons margarine or butter**
1 **cup chicken broth**
3 **tablespoons unsifted flour**
¼ **cup ReaLemon® Lemon Juice from Concentrate**
1 **teaspoon sugar**
2 **tablespoons chopped fresh chives**

Rinse chicken; pat dry. Combine ¼ cup flour, salt and pepper in plastic bag. Add chicken pieces, a few at a time, shaking to coat.

Cook chicken in hot margarine or butter in large skillet over medium-high heat 8 to 10 minutes or until tender and no longer pink, turning once. (Reduce heat as necessary during cooking to prevent overbrowning.) Remove from skillet, reserving any drippings. Keep warm.

For sauce, combine broth and 3 tablespoons flour in screw-top jar. Cover and shake well; add to skillet. Cook and stir until thickened and bubbly. Cook and stir 1 minute longer. Stir in ReaLemon and sugar; heat through.

Serve sauce over chicken. Sprinkle with chives.

Nutrition facts per serving: 197 cal., 7 g total fat (2 g sat. fat), 60 mg chol., 319 mg sodium, 8 g carbo., 0 g fiber, 23 g pro.

Spark It Up

It's a cinch to create tasty juices to serve with panbroiled chicken, beef or pork. Just squirt some ReaLemon into the skillet after removing the meat, then scrape up the crusty browned bits and spoon the juices over the meat.

chicken and vegetable stir-fry

Like stir-fries but not all the chopping and measuring usually called for? Frozen stir-fry vegetables and a quick-fix sauce make this one of the most work-free wok specialties ever (photo, pages 40–41).

Prep time: 10 minutes   **Cook time:** 8 to 11 minutes   **Makes:** 4 servings

½ cup water
⅓ cup apricot preserves
¼ cup ReaLime® Lime Juice
      from Concentrate
 1 tablespoon cornstarch
 1 tablespoon soy sauce
12 ounces skinless, boneless
      chicken breast strips for
      stir-frying
 2 cups chow mein noodles
 1 tablespoon cooking oil
 1 (16-ounce) package frozen
      broccoli stir-fry vegetables

Preheat oven to 350°. For sauce, combine water, apricot preserves, ReaLime, cornstarch and soy sauce in small bowl. Rinse chicken; pat dry. Set aside.

Place noodles in shallow baking pan; bake 5 minutes or until heated through.

Meanwhile, pour oil into wok or large skillet. (Add more oil as necessary during cooking.) Preheat over medium-high heat.

Stir-fry frozen vegetables in hot oil 2 to 3 minutes or until crisp-tender. Remove from wok. Add chicken; stir-fry 3 to 4 minutes or until chicken is no longer pink. Push chicken from center of wok.

Stir sauce; add to center of wok. Cook and stir until thickened and bubbly.

Return vegetables to wok. Cook and stir 1 to 2 minutes or until heated through. Serve immediately over noodles.

Nutrition facts per serving: 364 cal., 13 g total fat (2 g sat. fat), 45 mg chol., 425 mg sodium, 43 g carbo., 1 g fiber, 20 g pro. Daily values: 80% vit. A, 40% vit. C.

Stir-Fry Like a Pro

Stir-frying is easy and fast if you follow these simple pointers:

■ **No wok? Use a large, deep skillet.**

■ **Assemble and prepare all of the ingredients before you start to stir-fry. (If you like, do this up to 24 hours ahead and chill each ingredient separately.)**

■ **Preheat the oil, then test its hotness by adding a vegetable piece; if the piece sizzles, start stir-frying.**

chicken and pear stir-fry

The fruity apple and pear flavors lend a tempting sweetness to this intriguing entrée. Add the Romaine and Toasted Walnut Salad (recipe, page 62) and crusty sourdough bread to complete the meal.

Prep time: 15 minutes   **Cook time:** 12 to 17 minutes   **Makes:** 6 servings

¾ **cup apple juice**
¼ **cup ReaLemon® Lemon Juice from Concentrate**
2 **tablespoons hoisin sauce *or* barbecue sauce**
1 **tablespoon cornstarch**
1¼ **pounds skinless, boneless chicken breast strips for stir-frying**
1 **tablespoon cooking oil**
2 **cloves garlic, finely chopped**
1 **medium red onion, cut into wedges**
2 **medium pears, thinly sliced**
3 **to 4 cups hot cooked rice**

For sauce, combine apple juice, ReaLemon, hoisin or barbecue sauce and cornstarch in small bowl. Rinse chicken; pat dry. Set aside.

Pour oil into wok or very large skillet. (Add more oil as necessary during cooking.) Preheat over medium-high heat.

Stir-fry garlic in hot oil 15 seconds. Add onion; stir-fry 2 to 3 minutes or until crisp-tender. Remove from wok. Add half of the chicken; stir-fry 3 to 4 minutes or until chicken is no longer pink. Remove from wok. Stir-fry remaining chicken and remove from wok.

Stir sauce; add to wok. Cook and stir until thickened and bubbly. Return onion and chicken to wok. Cook and stir 1 to 2 minutes or until heated through.

Add pears. Cook and stir 1 to 2 minutes longer or until pears are heated through but still firm. Serve immediately over rice.

Nutrition facts per serving: 299 cal., 5 g total fat (1 g sat. fat), 50 mg chol., 154 mg sodium, 40 g carbo., 2 g fiber, 21 g pro.

Turkey Sausage
Vegetable Soup

baked apricot chicken

ReaLemon makes it easy to enhance the flavor of foods without adding fat. Case in point: the luscious, sweet-tart sauce on this easy entrée is fat free.

Prep time: 15 minutes   **Bake time:** 1 hour   **Makes:** 6 servings

1 **(12-ounce) jar apricot *or* peach preserves**
¼ **cup ReaLemon® Lemon Juice from Concentrate**
2 **teaspoons soy sauce**
½ **teaspoon salt**
2 **to 2½ pounds meaty chicken pieces (breasts, thighs and drumsticks)**
¾ **cup dry bread crumbs**
2 **tablespoons margarine *or* butter, melted**

Preheat oven to 350°. Combine apricot or peach preserves, ReaLemon, soy sauce and salt in shallow dish.

Skin and rinse chicken; pat dry. Coat chicken with apricot mixture; roll in bread crumbs. Set aside remaining apricot mixture. Place chicken in greased 13x9-inch baking dish; drizzle with margarine or butter.

Bake 1 hour or until tender and no longer pink. Bring reserved apricot mixture to a boil; cover and boil 1 minute. Serve with chicken.

Nutrition facts per serving: 368 cal., 9 g total fat (2 g sat. fat), 61 mg chol., 493 mg sodium, 50 g carbo., 1 g fiber, 22 g pro.

turkey sausage vegetable soup

Great flavor, varied textures and a confetti of color make for a winning supper that stirs together fast.

Prep time: 10 minutes   **Cook time:** 13 minutes   **Makes:** 4 servings

1 **(14½-ounce) can chicken broth**
1 **cup water**
½ **teaspoon dried Italian seasoning, crushed**
1 **cup packaged dried rotini (corkscrew) pasta**
2 **cups loose-pack frozen zucchini, carrots, cauliflower, lima beans and Italian green beans**
1 **(14½-ounce) can diced tomatoes with basil, garlic and oregano**
8 **ounces cooked smoked turkey sausage, halved lengthwise and sliced**
¼ **cup ReaLemon® Lemon Juice from Concentrate**
2 **teaspoons sugar**

Combine broth, water and Italian seasoning in large saucepan. Bring to a boil; add pasta. Reduce heat; cover and simmer 8 minutes.

Stir in frozen vegetables, tomatoes with juice, sausage, ReaLemon and sugar. Return to a boil. Reduce heat; cover and simmer 5 minutes longer or until vegetables and pasta are tender.

Nutrition facts per serving: 307 cal., 9 g total fat (0 g sat. fat), 30 mg chol., 1,444 mg sodium, 40 g carbo., 3 g fiber, 17 g pro. Daily values: 87% vit. A, 38% vit. C.

chicken with lemon-pesto pasta

This lemony version of pesto is a versatile ingredient indeed. Use any you have left over to top grilled fish or steaks. Or, stir it into a favorite vegetable soup for a burst of flavor.

Prep time: 25 minutes   **Cook time:** 8 to 10 minutes
Makes: 4 servings (about 1 cup pesto)

> 4   **medium skinless, boneless chicken breast halves (1 pound)**
> 1/4 **teaspoon salt**
> 1/4 **teaspoon cracked pepper**
> 2   **tablespoons margarine *or* butter**
> 1   **(9-ounce) package refrigerated linguine**
> 1/2 **cup Lemon-Spinach Pesto (recipe follows)**
>   **Toasted pine nuts, optional**

Rinse chicken; pat dry. Sprinkle with salt and pepper. Cook chicken in hot margarine or butter in large skillet over medium-high heat 8 to 10 minutes or until tender and no longer pink, turning once. (Reduce heat as necessary during cooking to prevent overbrowning.)

Meanwhile, cook linguine according to package directions; drain well. Add 1/2 cup Lemon-Spinach Pesto; toss gently to coat.

Divide pasta among dinner plates. Cut each chicken breast diagonally into 4 or 5 slices and fan out on top of pasta. Sprinkle with pine nuts if desired.

Nutrition facts per serving: 345 cal., 17 g total fat (4 g sat. fat), 87 mg chol., 490 mg sodium, 18 g carbo., 1 g fiber, 29 g pro. Daily values: 19% vit. A, 10% vit. C.

lemon-spinach pesto

Combine 2 cups lightly packed torn fresh *spinach leaves* or *parsley,* 1 cup lightly packed fresh *basil leaves,* 2/3 cup grated *Parmesan cheese,* 2 cloves *garlic,* quartered, and 1/4 teaspoon *salt* in food processor bowl. Cover and process until a paste forms. Gradually add 1/4 cup *ReaLemon® Lemon Juice from Concentrate* and 3 tablespoons *olive oil* or *cooking oil* with machine running. Cover and process until consistency of soft butter. Store leftover pesto in refrigerator up to 3 days or in freezer up to 3 months.

Keeping Herbs Fresh

To keep parsley and other herbs at their peak, trim the stem ends. Place them in a tall container of water, immersing the stems about 2 inches. Cover the leaves loosely with a plastic bag and store in the refrigerator.

tangy barbecued chicken sandwiches

Here's a sweet and tangy sandwich the whole family can enjoy.

Prep time: 15 minutes   **Cook time:** 12 to 14 minutes

Makes: 4 servings

4   **medium skinless, boneless chicken breast halves (1 pound)**
1   **cup water**
½   **cup ReaLemon® Lemon Juice from Concentrate**
¾   **cup barbecue sauce**
⅓   **to ½ cup ReaLemon® Lemon Juice from Concentrate**
2   **tablespoons molasses**
4   **hoagie buns, split**
     Green bell pepper slices *or* pickled jalapeño peppers, optional

Rinse chicken; pat dry. Combine water and ½ cup ReaLemon in large skillet. Add chicken.

Bring to a boil. Reduce heat; cover and simmer 12 to 14 minutes or until chicken is tender and no longer pink. Drain well. Shred chicken with 2 forks.

Combine barbecue sauce, ⅓ to ½ cup ReaLemon and molasses in medium-sized saucepan. Bring to a boil. Reduce heat; stir in shredded chicken and heat through.

Serve on buns with green pepper slices or jalapeño peppers if desired.

Nutrition facts per serving: 611 cal., 9 g total fat (2 g sat. fat), 59 mg chol., 1,514 mg sodium, 99 g carbo., 4 g fiber, 34 g pro.

Figuring Nutrition

To help you keep track of what you eat, each recipe in this book lists the nutrient values for one serving, as well as the daily values for vitamins **A** and **C** when the recipe provides 10% or more of the recommended daily values. However, vitamin **C** amounts may vary due to heat applied during cooking.

When analyzing the recipes, if there is a choice of ingredients or a range in servings, the first ingredient or serving size listed is used in the analysis. Also, optional ingredients are omitted in the analysis. Numbers are rounded to the nearest whole number.

mexican pork chops with couscous

Dinnertime dips south of the border with these sassy salsa-topped chops.

Prep time: 15 minutes   **Cook time:** 6 to 8 minutes   **Makes:** 4 servings

- **4 pork loin rib chops, cut ¾ inch thick**
- **2 tablespoons cooking oil**
- **1 (8-ounce) can tomato sauce**
- **1 cup salsa**
- **1 cup frozen whole kernel corn**
- **¼ cup ReaLime® Lime Juice from Concentrate**
- **1 tablespoon cold water**
- **1 teaspoon cornstarch**
- **2 cups hot cooked couscous**

Trim fat from chops. Lightly sprinkle both sides with *salt* and *pepper*. Cook chops in hot oil in large skillet over medium-high heat 4 minutes or until brown, turning once. Drain fat.

Add tomato sauce, salsa, corn and ReaLime. Bring to a boil. Reduce heat; cover and simmer 6 to 8 minutes or until chops are no longer pink and juices run clear. Remove chops; keep warm.

For sauce, combine water and cornstarch in small bowl; stir into tomato mixture. Cook and stir until thickened and bubbly. Cook and stir 2 minutes longer.

Spoon sauce over pork chops and couscous. Garnish with green bell pepper strips and fresh cilantro sprigs if desired.

Nutrition facts per serving: 496 cal., 21 g total fat (5 g sat. fat), 112 mg chol., 676 mg sodium, 38 g carbo., 5 g fiber, 42 g pro. Daily values: 14% vit. A, 27% vit. C.

lemon-pepper fettuccine and ham

Lemon and pepper is one of the most exciting flavor combinations to become popular in recent years. Here, its peppery tartness provides a great contrast to the creamy, ultra-smooth pasta sauce.

Prep time: 15 minutes   **Cook time:** 5 minutes   **Makes:** 4 servings

1 **(9-ounce) package refrigerated fettuccine**
1½ **cups broccoli flowerets**
1 **(8-ounce) tub cream cheese with chive and onion**
¼ **cup ReaLemon® Lemon Juice from Concentrate**
8 **ounces cooked ham, cut into cubes (1½ cups)**
2 **tablespoons milk**
¼ **teaspoon pepper**
   Finely shredded *or* grated Parmesan cheese, optional

Cook fettuccine in salted water in large saucepan according to package directions, adding broccoli last 3 minutes. Drain; return to saucepan.

Meanwhile, cook and stir cream cheese in medium-sized saucepan over low heat until softened. Gradually stir in ReaLemon until smooth. Stir in ham, milk and pepper. Cook and stir until heated through.

Pour over pasta mixture; toss gently to coat. Before serving, sprinkle with Parmesan cheese if desired.

Nutrition facts per serving: 364 cal., 20 g total fat (11 g sat. fat), 112 mg chol., 1,017 mg sodium, 21 g carbo., 2 g fiber, 22 g pro. Daily values: 20% vit. A, 26% vit. C.

Marinated Bean Salad
(recipe, page 67)

Beef Fajitas

beef fajitas

To add a festive touch, place the salsa, sour cream and cheese in pretty bowls on the table. Then, bring the beef and vegetable mixture to the table still sizzling in the skillet—just the way restaurants do—and let everyone fill and roll up their own creations.

Prep time: 10 minutes
Cook time: 9 to 13 minutes
Marinate time: 30 minutes
Makes: 4 servings

1	**pound boneless beef strips for stir-frying**
⅓	**cup ReaLime® Lime Juice from Concentrate**
¼	**cup salsa**
3	**tablespoons cooking oil**
8	**(7-inch) flour tortillas**
½	**(16-ounce) package frozen pepper stir-fry vegetables**
	Salsa *or* chopped tomatoes, optional
	Dairy sour cream, optional
	Shredded cheddar, Monterey Jack *or* Monterey Jack cheese with jalapeño peppers, optional

Place beef in plastic bag set in bowl. For marinade, combine ReaLime, salsa and 2 tablespoons of the oil in small bowl. Pour over beef; seal bag. Marinate at room temperature 30 minutes or in refrigerator 6 to 24 hours, turning occasionally.

Preheat oven to 350°. Wrap tortillas in foil. Bake 10 minutes or until warm. Meanwhile, drain meat, reserving marinade.

Pour remaining 1 tablespoon oil into large skillet. (Add more oil as necessary during cooking.) Preheat over medium-high heat. Stir-fry frozen vegetables in hot oil 2 to 3 minutes or until crisp-tender. Remove from skillet; drain liquid.

Add half of the beef to skillet; stir-fry 3 to 4 minutes or until desired doneness. Remove from skillet. Stir-fry remaining beef. Return beef and vegetables to skillet; add marinade. Cook and stir 1 to 2 minutes or until heated through.

Fill tortillas with beef mixture. Top with salsa or tomatoes, sour cream and cheese if desired. Garnish with fresh cilantro sprigs if desired.

Nutrition facts per serving: 499 cal., 25 g total fat (7 g sat. fat), 76 mg chol., 392 mg sodium, 36 g carbo., 1 g fiber, 31 g pro. Daily values: 40% vit. A, 24% vit. C.

beef stir-fry

Orzo, a rice-shaped pasta, makes a nice change of pace from rice, the usual stir-fry standby.

Prep time: 10 minutes   **Cook time:** 9 to 11 minutes   **Makes:** 4 servings

¾ cup water
¼ cup ReaLemon® Lemon Juice
     from Concentrate
2 tablespoons cornstarch
1 tablespoon sugar
1 tablespoon soy sauce
1 teaspoon instant beef
     bouillon granules
     Several drops bottled hot
     pepper sauce
1 tablespoon cooking oil
2 cloves garlic, finely chopped
4 cups precut fresh
     vegetables for stir-frying
     (tip, below)
12 ounces boneless beef strips
     for stir-frying
1 small tomato, cut into thin
     wedges
2 to 3 cups hot cooked orzo
     or rice

For sauce, combine water, ReaLemon, cornstarch, sugar, soy sauce, bouillon granules and pepper sauce in small bowl. Set aside.

Pour oil into wok or very large skillet. (Add more oil as necessary during cooking.) Preheat over medium-high heat.

Stir-fry garlic in hot oil 15 seconds. Add vegetables; stir-fry 3 to 4 minutes or until crisp-tender. Remove from wok. Add beef; stir-fry 3 to 4 minutes or until desired doneness. Push beef from center of wok.

Stir sauce; add to center of wok. Cook and stir until thickened and bubbly. Return vegetables to wok; add tomato. Cook and stir 1 minute or until heated through.

Serve immediately over orzo or rice.

Nutrition facts per serving: 352 cal., 12 g total fat (4 g sat. fat), 57 mg chol., 536 mg sodium, 36 g carbo., 4 g fiber, 25 g pro. Daily values: 85% vit. A, 57% vit. C.

Opt for Precut Veggies

Save time and effort by scouting your supermarket produce section for vegetables that are already peeled, cut up and ready to use. To make sure they cook uniformly, cut any larger ones into 1-inch pieces so all of the vegetables are of similar size.

saucy white beans and tomatoes

Cannellini beans give this meatless main dish its fullness. If you like, add cooked smoked turkey sausage to satisfy heartier appetites.

Prep time: 15 minutes   **Cook time:** 5 minutes   **Makes:** 4 servings

Uncooked quick-cooking brown rice for 4 servings
- 1 **medium carrot, chopped**
- 1 **medium onion, chopped**
- 1 **clove garlic, finely chopped**
- 1 **tablespoon cooking oil**
- 1 **(19- or 15-ounce) can white kidney (cannellini) beans or great northern beans, rinsed and drained**
- 1 **(14½-ounce) can Mexican-style stewed tomatoes**
- ¼ **cup ReaLemon® Lemon Juice from Concentrate**

Cook rice according to package directions. Meanwhile, cook carrot, onion and garlic in hot oil in large skillet until tender. Stir in beans, tomatoes with juice and ReaLemon.

Bring to a boil. Reduce heat; simmer 5 minutes or until desired consistency. Serve over rice.

Nutrition facts per serving: 246 cal., 5 g total fat (1 g sat. fat), 0 mg chol., 509 mg sodium, 49 g carbo., 9 g fiber, 10 g pro. Daily values: 46% vit. A, 13% vit. C.

almond salmon and green beans

Green beans topped with buttery almonds are an all-time favorite. Here, the combo adds elegance to succulent salmon.

Prep time: 10 minutes   **Cook time:** 10 to 12 minutes   **Makes:** 4 servings

- 4 **(6-ounce) fresh or thawed frozen salmon, swordfish or shark steaks, cut 1 inch thick**
- ¼ **cup sliced almonds**
- 3 **tablespoons butter or margarine**
- 1 **(9-ounce) package refrigerated fettuccine**
- 1 **(9-ounce) package frozen cut green beans**
- ¼ **cup ReaLemon® Lemon Juice from Concentrate**

Rinse fish; pat dry. Set aside. Cook and stir almonds in 2 tablespoons of the hot butter or margarine in large skillet over medium heat 2 to 3 minutes or until lightly browned. Using a slotted spoon, remove from skillet.

Add fish. Cook 10 to 12 minutes or until fish flakes easily when tested with a fork, turning once. Remove from skillet.

Meanwhile, cook fettuccine with green beans according to package directions for pasta. Drain and toss with remaining 1 tablespoon butter or margarine.

Add ReaLemon to skillet; cook until heated through. Remove from heat. Stir in almonds.

Serve fish on top of fettuccine mixture and drizzle with lemon mixture.

Nutrition facts per serving: 376 cal., 19 g total fat (7 g sat. fat), 75 mg chol., 204 mg sodium, 22 g carbo., 1 g fiber, 30 g pro. Daily value: 15% vit. A.

fish steaks with lemon-mustard sauce

The poaching juices add extra richness to the velvety sauce. Add a touch of mustard and cream, and the dish becomes reminiscent of the simple-yet-stunning fare found in informal French bistros.

Prep time: 15 minutes   **Cook time:** 8 to 12 minutes   **Makes:** 6 servings

6 (4-ounce) fresh *or* thawed
    frozen halibut, sea bass *or*
    tuna steaks, cut 1 inch
    thick
¾ cup water
½ cup chicken broth
⅓ cup ReaLemon® Lemon Juice
    from Concentrate
1 tablespoon butter *or*
    margarine
½ cup half-and-half *or* light
    cream
2 tablespoons unsifted flour
1 tablespoon prepared *or*
    Dijon mustard
1 tablespoon chopped fresh
    chives

Rinse fish; pat dry. Combine water, broth and ReaLemon in large skillet. Bring to a boil. Reduce heat; carefully add fish. Cover and simmer 8 to 12 minutes or until fish flakes easily when tested with a fork. Remove from skillet; keep warm.

Pour cooking liquid through fine-mesh sieve; discard solids. Return 1 cup cooking liquid to skillet. Stir in butter or margarine. Gradually stir half-and-half or cream into flour; stir into cooking liquid.

Cook and stir over medium heat until slightly thickened and bubbly (mixture may appear curdled at first). Stir in mustard; cook and stir 1 minute longer. Stir in chopped chives. Serve with fish. Garnish with whole fresh chives if desired.

Nutrition facts per serving: 184 cal., 7 g total fat (3 g sat. fat), 49 mg chol., 197 mg sodium, 4 g carbo., 0 g fiber, 25 g pro.

Fish-Buying Finesse

When selecting fresh fish, choose only fish that has a sweet, mild smell, not a strong odor. Look for fillets or steaks that appear moist and recently cut. It's best to cook the fish the same day you buy it. If that's not possible, store it in the coldest part of the refrigerator for up to 2 days, or freeze it.

herb-buttered fish fillets

This simple recipe is perfect for glistening fresh fish, for it won't mask its delicate flavor.

Prep time: 10 minutes   **Cook time:** 8 to 12 minutes   **Makes:** 6 servings

1½ **pounds fresh *or* thawed frozen halibut, swordfish *or* salmon fillets, 1 inch thick**
¼ **cup ReaLime® Lime Juice from Concentrate**
3 **tablespoons butter *or* margarine**
1 **tablespoon chopped fresh parsley**
1 **teaspoon chopped fresh dill**

Rinse fish; pat dry. Cut into 6 serving-size pieces if necessary. Place fish on greased unheated rack of broiler pan.

Combine ReaLime and butter or margarine in small saucepan. Cook over low heat until butter melts. Remove from heat. Stir in parsley and dill. Set aside ¼ cup lime mixture.

Brush fish with some of the remaining lime mixture. Sprinkle with *salt* and *pepper.* Broil 4 inches from heat 5 minutes. Turn; brush with remaining lime mixture. Broil 3 to 7 minutes longer or until fish flakes easily when tested with a fork.

Before serving, drizzle reserved lime mixture over fish.

Nutrition facts per serving: 176 cal., 8 g total fat (4 g sat. fat), 52 mg chol., 121 mg sodium, 1 g carbo., 0 g fiber, 24 g pro. Daily value: 10% vit. A.

fish fillets with sour cream sauce

Top a fish that's poached to perfection in minutes with a sauce that stirs together in seconds, and you have a delicious recipe that's perfect for today's hassle-free cooking.

Prep time: 15 minutes   **Cook time:** 6 to 9 minutes   **Makes:** 6 servings

⅓ **cup dairy sour cream**
¼ **cup mayonnaise *or* salad dressing**
2 **tablespoons thinly sliced green onion**
½ **teaspoon bottled roasted garlic**
¼ **teaspoon dried thyme, crushed**
¼ **cup ReaLemon® Lemon Juice from Concentrate**
1½ **pounds fresh *or* thawed frozen skinless salmon, orange roughy *or* other fish fillets, ¾ inch thick**
1 **teaspoon instant chicken bouillon granules**

For sauce, combine sour cream, mayonnaise or salad dressing, green onion, roasted garlic and thyme in small bowl. Stir in 2 tablespoons of the ReaLemon; set aside.

Rinse fish; pat dry. Cut into 6 serving-size pieces if necessary. Bring 1 cup *water* to a boil in very large skillet; stir in bouillon granules and remaining 2 tablespoons ReaLemon. Reduce heat; carefully add fish. Cover and simmer 6 to 9 minutes or until fish flakes easily when tested with a fork. Remove fish. Serve with sauce.

Nutrition facts per serving: 200 cal., 15 g total fat (4 g sat. fat), 29 mg chol., 199 mg sodium, 1 g carbo., 0 g fiber, 17 g pro.

shrimp and asparagus stir-fry

Let the sun shine in! The bright, light flavors of the seafood and asparagus are further sparked by an unmistakable burst of sunny lemon flavor.

Prep time: 20 minutes   **Cook time:** 10 to 11 minutes
Makes: 4 to 6 servings

1	cup water
⅓	cup ReaLemon® Lemon Juice from Concentrate
3	tablespoons sugar
2	tablespoons cornstarch
2	teaspoons instant chicken bouillon granules
1	pound fresh *or* thawed frozen peeled and deveined medium shrimp
1	tablespoon cooking oil
2	cloves garlic, finely chopped
1	pound fresh asparagus, trimmed and bias-cut into 1-inch pieces, *or* 1 (10-ounce) package thawed frozen cut asparagus
1½	cups sliced fresh mushrooms
3	cups hot cooked rice

For sauce, combine water, ReaLemon, sugar, cornstarch and bouillon granules in small bowl. Rinse shrimp; pat dry. Set aside.

Pour oil into wok or large skillet. (Add more oil as necessary during cooking.) Preheat over medium-high heat.

Stir-fry garlic in hot oil 15 seconds. Add asparagus; stir-fry 2 minutes. Add mushrooms; stir-fry 2 minutes longer or until crisp-tender. Remove from wok. Add shrimp; stir-fry 2 to 3 minutes or until shrimp turn pink. Push shrimp from center of wok.

Stir sauce; add to center of wok. Cook and stir until thickened and bubbly. Return vegetables to wok. Cook and stir 1 minute or until heated through.

Serve immediately over rice.

Nutrition facts per serving: 357 cal., 5 g total fat (1 g sat. fat), 174 mg chol., 661 mg sodium, 53 g carbo., 2 g fiber, 25 g pro. Daily values: 13% vit. A, 34% vit. C.

Banish Garlic Odor

To rid your hands of garlic odor, wash your hands in cold water and table salt. Rinse and then wash them again in warm water with hand soap and a splash of ReaLemon.

Tortellini-Asparagus Salad
(recipe, page 66)

refreshing
salads & sides

Watch out! These sensational salads and sides are sure to steal the show. That's because each is infused with just the right touch of ReaLemon or ReaLime to add a distinctive tang and a burst of flavor that always transcends the ordinary.

Tomato Salad with
Honey-Lime Vinaigrette
(recipe, page 62)

tomato salad with honey-lime vinaigrette

This honey of a dressing turns vine-ripened tomatoes or any combination of fresh salad greens into a masterpiece (photo, pages 60–61).

Prep time: 15 minutes   **Makes:** 4 servings

  4 **cups shredded spinach (6 ounces)**
  3 **medium red *and/or* yellow tomatoes**
  ¼ **cup ReaLime® Lime Juice from Concentrate**
  ¼ **cup olive oil *or* cooking oil**
  2 **tablespoons honey**
  2 **cloves garlic, finely chopped**
  ¼ **teaspoon salt**
  ⅛ **teaspoon pepper**
  I **large shallot, thinly sliced**

Divide spinach among salad plates. Cut each tomato into wedges; divide wedges among plates.

For dressing, combine ReaLime, oil, honey, garlic, salt and pepper in screw-top jar. Cover and shake well. Drizzle over salads. Sprinkle with shallot.

Nutrition facts per serving: 191 cal., 14 g total fat (2 g sat. fat), 0 mg chol., 189 mg sodium, 17 g carbo., 3 g fiber, 3 g pro. Daily values: 46% vit. A, 58% vit. C.

romaine and toasted walnut salad

Looking for a special, new salad to add to your repertoire? This is it (photo, pages 26–27)!

Prep time: 25 minutes   **Makes:** 8 servings

 10 **cups torn romaine (I medium head)**
  6 **Italian plum tomatoes, cut into wedges**
  I **small cucumber, thinly sliced**
  ⅓ **cup shredded carrot**
  ¼ **cup ReaLemon® Lemon Juice from Concentrate**
  ¼ **cup olive oil**
  2 **tablespoons honey**
  I **tablespoon red wine vinegar**
  ½ **teaspoon dry mustard**
  ¼ **teaspoon salt**
  ⅛ **teaspoon pepper**
  ½ **cup walnut pieces, toasted**

Combine romaine, tomatoes, cucumber and carrot in large salad bowl.

For dressing, combine ReaLemon, oil, honey, vinegar, mustard, salt and pepper in screw-top jar. Cover and shake well.

Pour over romaine mixture; toss gently to coat. Sprinkle with walnuts.

Nutrition facts per serving: 151 cal., 12 g total fat (1 g sat. fat), 0 mg chol., 81 mg sodium, 11 g carbo., 2 g fiber, 3 g pro. Daily values: 34% vit. A, 48% vit. C.

chili barley toss

These days, restaurants are serving barley as a refreshing alternative to rice. The creative fusion of flavors and textures in this recipe would fit right into a bistro menu.

Prep time: 10 minutes **Cook time:** 12 minutes **Cool time:** 10 minutes
Chill time: 4 to 24 hours **Makes:** 8 to 10 servings

1¼ **cups chicken broth**
1 **teaspoon chili powder**
⅔ **cup uncooked quick-cooking barley**
¾ **cup frozen whole kernel corn**
1 **(15-ounce) can black beans, rinsed and drained**
1 **(4-ounce) can diced green chili peppers**
¼ **cup sliced green onions**
¼ **cup ReaLemon® Lemon Juice from Concentrate**
¼ **cup salad oil**
1 **teaspoon sugar**
½ **teaspoon ground cumin**
¼ **teaspoon black pepper**
2 **medium tomatoes, seeded and chopped**
2 **tablespoons chopped fresh cilantro**

Combine broth and chili powder in medium-sized saucepan. Bring to a boil. Stir in barley; return to a boil. Reduce heat; cover and simmer 10 minutes.

Add corn; return to a boil. Reduce heat; cover and simmer 2 minutes longer. Remove from heat. Cool.

Transfer to large bowl. Stir in beans, chili peppers and green onions.

Meanwhile, for dressing, combine ReaLemon, oil, sugar, cumin and black pepper in screw-top jar. Cover and shake well. Pour over barley mixture; toss gently to coat. Chill 4 to 24 hours.

Before serving, stir in tomatoes and cilantro.

Nutrition facts per serving: 185 cal., 8 g total fat (1 g sat. fat), 0 mg chol., 302 mg sodium, 25 g carbo., 4 g fiber, 7 g pro. Daily values: 4% vit. A, 22% vit. C.

Intriguing Salad Greens

With the rich array of lettuces and greens on the market these days, you can select varieties for color and for sharp and sweet tastes. Consider smooth-textured Bibb, light green Boston, crunchy romaine and red and green leaf lettuce. They mix nicely with specialty greens such as tangy arugula, bitter radicchio and peppery watercress. Don't forget prewashed and cut greens, packaged in plastic bags; they've expanded our choices and sliced salad making to seconds.

honey-mustard slaw

Everyone needs a good coleslaw recipe, and you can't go wrong with this zesty version.

Prep time: 10 minutes   **Chill time:** 1 to 2 hours   **Makes:** 8 servings

8 **cups packaged shredded cabbage with carrot (coleslaw mix)**
1 **medium apple, chopped**
¼ **cup thinly sliced green onions**
⅓ **cup ReaLemon® Lemon Juice from Concentrate**
¼ **cup salad oil**
2 **tablespoons honey**
1 **tablespoon brown mustard**
¼ **teaspoon salt**
¼ **teaspoon pepper**

Combine shredded cabbage with carrot, apple and sliced green onions in large bowl.

For dressing, combine ReaLemon, oil, honey, mustard, salt and pepper in screw-top jar. Cover and shake well.

Pour over cabbage mixture; toss gently to coat. Chill 1 to 2 hours. Garnish with carrot curls and green onion tops if desired.

Nutrition facts per serving: 116 cal., 7 g total fat (1 g sat. fat), 0 mg chol., 113 mg sodium, 13 g carbo., 2 g fiber, 1 g pro. Daily values: 40% vit. A, 71% vit. C.

tabbouleh

For a no-oven supper on a hot summer's night, serve this refreshing salad with sliced deli meats, crusty country-style bread and Lemon-Lime Iced Tea (recipe, page 93).

Prep time: 15 minutes   **Chill time:** 4 to 24 hours   **Makes:** 6 servings

¾   **cup uncooked bulgur**
1   **(8¾-ounce) can red kidney beans, rinsed and drained**
½   **cup chopped seeded cucumber**
½   **cup chopped fresh parsley**
¼   **cup finely chopped onion**
¼   **cup ReaLemon® Lemon Juice from Concentrate**
¼   **cup olive oil or salad oil**
1   **tablespoon chopped fresh mint**
1   **teaspoon dried basil, crushed**
¼   **teaspoon salt**
⅛   **teaspoon pepper**
8   **cherry tomatoes, quartered**

Place bulgur in strainer; rinse with cold water and drain. Combine bulgur, beans, cucumber, parsley and onion in medium-sized bowl.

For dressing, combine ReaLemon, oil, mint, basil, salt and pepper in screw-top jar. Cover and shake well. Pour over bulgur mixture; toss gently to coat. Chill 4 to 24 hours.

Before serving, stir in tomatoes.

Nutrition facts per serving: 179 cal., 9 g total fat (1 g sat. fat), 0 mg chol., 157 mg sodium, 22 g carbo., 6 g fiber, 5 g pro. Daily value: 23% vit. C.

tortellini-asparagus salad

Make this substantial salad in the morning, and you're only grilled chicken away from a fun backyard supper tonight (photo, pages 60–61).

Prep time: 15 minutes   **Chill time:** 2 to 8 hours   **Makes:** 6 servings

1 **(9-ounce) package refrigerated cheese tortellini**
8 **ounces fresh asparagus, trimmed and cut into 2-inch pieces (2 cups)**
½ **cup bottled ranch salad dressing**
¼ **cup ReaLime® Lime Juice from Concentrate**
2 **tablespoons grated Parmesan cheese**
   Cracked pepper

Cook tortellini with asparagus in large saucepan according to package directions for pasta. Drain.

Meanwhile, for dressing, combine ranch dressing, ReaLime and Parmesan cheese in large bowl. Add pasta mixture; toss gently to coat. Chill 2 to 8 hours.

Before serving, sprinkle with pepper.

Nutrition facts per serving: 220 cal., 11 g total fat (2 g sat. fat), 27 mg chol., 326 mg sodium, 22 g carbo., 0 g fiber, 9 g pro. Daily value: 10% vit. C.

wild rice salad

Wild rice—a most elegant grain—gets a royal treatment with this Asian-spiced, fruit-studded salad.

Prep time: 15 minutes   **Cook time:** 40 minutes
Chill time: 4 to 8 hours   **Makes:** 8 servings

¾ **cup uncooked wild rice**
2 **cups water**
¼ **cup ReaLemon® Lemon Juice from Concentrate**
2 **tablespoons salad oil**
2 **tablespoons soy sauce**
1 **teaspoon sugar**
¼ **teaspoon ground ginger**
¼ **teaspoon toasted sesame oil, optional**
⅛ **teaspoon salt**
1 **(11-ounce) can mandarin orange sections, drained**
½ **(8-ounce) can sliced water chestnuts, drained (½ cup)**
   Romaine leaves

Place wild rice in strainer; rinse with cold water and drain. Combine wild rice and 2 cups water in medium-sized saucepan. Bring to a boil. Reduce heat; cover and simmer 40 minutes or until rice is just tender. Drain any liquid. Transfer rice to large bowl.

For dressing, combine ReaLemon, salad oil, soy sauce, sugar, ginger, sesame oil if desired and salt in screw-top jar. Cover and shake well. Pour over wild rice; toss gently to coat. Chill 4 to 8 hours.

Before serving, gently fold in mandarin oranges and water chestnuts. Serve on romaine.

Nutrition facts per serving: 115 cal., 4 g total fat (1 g sat. fat), 0 mg chol., 299 mg sodium, 19 g carbo., 0 g fiber, 3 g pro.

marinated bean salad

Canned beans cut soaking and cooking time completely in this fast and flavorful fiber-packed salad (photo, page 52).

Prep time: 15 minutes   **Chill time:** 2 to 24 hours   **Makes:** 8 servings

1   (15-ounce) can black beans, rinsed and drained
1   (15-ounce) can great northern beans, rinsed and drained
1   (14½-ounce) can cut green beans, rinsed and drained
1   small red *or* green bell pepper, chopped
1   small sweet onion, halved lengthwise and thinly sliced
⅓   cup ReaLemon® Lemon Juice from Concentrate
¼   cup salad oil
1   tablespoon sugar
1   clove garlic, finely chopped
¼   teaspoon salt
¼   teaspoon black pepper
¼   teaspoon dried dillweed, optional

Combine beans, bell pepper and onion in large bowl. For dressing, combine ReaLemon, oil, sugar, garlic, salt, black pepper and dillweed if desired in screw-top jar. Cover and shake well. Pour over bean mixture; toss gently to coat.

Chill 2 to 24 hours, stirring occasionally. Serve using a slotted spoon. Garnish with romaine leaves if desired.

Nutrition facts per serving: 160 cal., 7 g total fat (1 g sat. fat), 0 mg chol., 309 mg sodium, 20 g carbo., 5 g fiber, 7 g pro. Daily values: 11% vit. A, 37% vit. C.

marinated mushrooms and zucchini

What's summer without its windfall of colorful, crunchy zucchini and tender yellow squash? This zippy recipe superbly showcases these favorite farmer's-market finds.

Prep time: 15 minutes   **Marinate time:** 4 to 8 hours   **Makes:** 6 servings

8   ounces fresh button, cremini *or* chanterelle mushrooms, quartered
1   medium zucchini, halved lengthwise and sliced ¼ inch thick
1   medium yellow summer squash, halved lengthwise and sliced ¼ inch thick
¼   cup ReaLemon® Lemon Juice from Concentrate
¼   cup salad oil
1   tablespoon Dijon mustard
1   teaspoon sugar
½   teaspoon dried basil, crushed
¼   teaspoon salt
¼   teaspoon cracked pepper

Combine mushrooms, zucchini and yellow squash in medium-sized bowl.

For marinade, combine ReaLemon, oil, mustard, sugar, basil, salt and pepper in screw-top jar. Cover and shake well. Pour over mushroom mixture.

Marinate in refrigerator 4 to 8 hours, stirring twice. Serve using a slotted spoon.

Nutrition facts per serving: 105 cal., 10 g total fat (1 g sat. fat), 0 mg chol., 157 mg sodium, 5 g carbo., 1 g fiber, 2 g pro. Daily value: 14% vit. C.

potato salad niçoise

Although Niçoise salad comes in many versions, this one features a burst of ReaLime to enliven the flavors. To make it a main-dish salad, add tuna and hard-cooked eggs.

Prep time: 20 minutes   **Cook time:** 15 to 20 minutes   **Makes:** 6 serving

12	**ounces fresh whole green beans, trimmed, *or* 1 (9-ounce) package frozen whole green beans**
12	**ounces tiny new potatoes, halved**
1	**medium onion, chopped**
2	**tablespoons olive oil *or* salad oil**
1	**tablespoon sugar**
2	**teaspoons cornstarch**
½	**teaspoon salt**
½	**teaspoon celery seed**
¼	**teaspoon pepper**
⅓	**cup water**
¼	**cup ReaLime® Lime Juice from Concentrate**
8	**cups torn mixed greens**
½	**cup halved cherry tomatoes**
2	**tablespoons sliced pitted ripe olives**

Cook fresh green beans with potatoes in boiling water in large covered saucepan 15 to 20 minutes or until just tender. (If using frozen beans, add during last 5 minutes.) Drain; return to saucepan.

Meanwhile, cook onion in hot oil in medium-sized saucepan until tender. Stir in sugar, cornstarch, salt, celery seed and pepper. Add water and ReaLime.

Cook and stir until slightly thickened and bubbly. Cook and stir 2 minutes longer. Pour over potato mixture; toss gently to coat.

Divide greens among 6 salad plates. Top with potato mixture, tomatoes and olives.

Nutrition facts per serving: 150 cal., 5 g total fat (1 g sat. fat), 0 mg chol., 207 mg sodium, 24 g carbo., 3 g fiber, 4 g pro. Daily value: 22% vit. C.

Prevent Browning Fruit

To keep fruit, such as apples, pears, peaches and bananas (or potatoes), from turning brown when cut, brush the pieces with ReaLemon or dip them into a mixture of ReaLemon and water.

lemon rice with peas

Consider this a versatile side dish—it will go with just about anything!

Prep time: 15 minutes **Cook time:** 15 to 18 minutes
Stand time: 5 minutes **Makes:** 6 servings

1½ **cups uncooked long grain rice**
¼ **teaspoon dried thyme, crushed**
2 **tablespoons margarine**
1 **(14½-ounce) can chicken broth**
1¼ **cups water**
¼ **cup ReaLemon® Lemon Juice from Concentrate**
¼ **teaspoon pepper**
¾ **cup frozen peas**
2 **tablespoons sliced almonds, toasted**

Cook and stir rice and thyme in hot margarine in medium-sized saucepan 5 minutes or until rice is lightly golden. Carefully stir in broth, water, ReaLemon and pepper.

Bring to a boil. Reduce heat; cover and simmer 15 to 18 minutes or until rice is tender and liquid is absorbed. Remove from heat. Stir in peas. Cover and let stand 5 minutes. Before serving, sprinkle with almonds.

Nutrition facts per serving: 244 cal., 6 g total fat (1 g sat. fat), 0 mg chol., 282 mg sodium, 41 g carbo., 1 g fiber, 6 g pro.

zesty summer squash and pasta

Take a tip from the Italians: Tossing (rather than topping) the pasta with the sauce makes for a more balanced dish. Try the technique in this delicious side dish (photo, pages 6–7).

Prep time: 15 minutes **Cook time:** 10 minutes **Makes:** 6 servings

4 **ounces packaged dried bow-tie pasta (2 cups)**
1 **medium zucchini, thinly sliced (1¼ cups)**
1 **medium yellow summer squash, thinly sliced (1¼ cups)**
¼ **cup finely chopped shallots**
2 **tablespoons margarine**
¾ **cup chicken broth**
¼ **cup ReaLemon® Lemon Juice from Concentrate**
1 **tablespoon cornstarch**
1 **tablespoon honey**
½ **teaspoon dried dillweed**
⅛ **teaspoon salt**
2 **tablespoons finely shredded Parmesan cheese**

Cook pasta in large saucepan according to package directions, adding zucchini and yellow squash last 3 minutes. Drain; return to saucepan.

Meanwhile, cook shallots in hot margarine in small saucepan until tender. Combine broth, ReaLemon, cornstarch, honey, dillweed and salt in small bowl; add to shallots. Cook and stir until thickened and bubbly. Cook and stir 2 minutes longer. Pour over pasta mixture; toss gently to coat.

Before serving, sprinkle with Parmesan cheese.

Nutrition facts per serving: 144 cal., 5 g total fat (1 g sat. fat), 18 mg chol., 220 mg sodium, 20 g carbo., 1 g fiber, 4 g pro. Daily value: 14% vit. A.

lemony roasted vegetables

To bring something new to the table, try the fennel option. Its licorice-like bite blends well with the mellow flavors of the other root vegetables.

Prep time: 20 minutes   **Bake time:** 30 minutes   **Makes:** 6 to 8 servings

1   **pound tiny new potatoes, halved, *or* 3 medium potatoes, cut into 1½-inch pieces**

3   **stalks celery, bias-sliced ½ inch thick, *or* 1 medium fennel bulb, cut into wedges**

4   **small carrots, bias-cut into 1½-inch pieces**

1   **large onion, cut into wedges**

¼   **cup ReaLemon® Lemon Juice from Concentrate**

2   **tablespoons olive oil**

1   **teaspoon dried rosemary, crushed**

¼   **teaspoon salt**

¼   **teaspoon cracked pepper**

Preheat oven to 450°. Place potatoes, celery or fennel, carrots and onion in greased shallow roasting pan.

Combine ReaLemon, oil, rosemary, salt and pepper in small bowl. Drizzle over vegetables, tossing to coat.

Bake 30 minutes or until potatoes and onion wedges are tender, stirring once.

Nutrition facts per serving: 152 cal., 5 g total fat (1 g sat. fat), 0 mg chol., 152 mg sodium, 26 g carbo., 3 g fiber, 3 g pro. Daily values: 85% vit. A, 19% vit. C.

stylish sweets

Here's an irresistible dessert collection, with choices ranging from the classic **Key Lime Pie** to the contemporary **Lime-Papaya Sorbet**. Sound difficult? No way! All recipes are made easier and consistently delicious thanks to ReaLemon.

Blueberry Crumb Cake
(recipe, page 75)

Lemony Fruit Bowl
(recipe, page 74)

Lemon Crumb Bars
(recipe, page 74)

lemony fruit bowl

Looking for a sprightly finish to a rich meal? Here's the answer (photo, pages 72–73)!

Prep time: 20 minutes   **Chill time:** 2 to 4 hours   **Makes:** 8 servings

2	**medium apples *and/or* pears, coarsely chopped**
1½	**cups strawberries, halved**
1½	**cups honeydew melon *or* cantaloupe balls**
1½	**cups seedless grapes**
¼	**cup honey**
¼	**cup ReaLemon® Lemon Juice from Concentrate**
¼	**cup orange juice**
1	**tablespoon chopped fresh mint**
2	**tablespoons sliced almonds, toasted**

Combine apples and/or pears, strawberries, melon balls and grapes in large bowl.

Combine honey, ReaLemon, orange juice and mint in small bowl. Pour over fruit; toss gently to coat. Chill 2 to 4 hours.

Before serving, sprinkle with almonds.

Nutrition facts per serving: 111 cal., 2 g total fat (0 g sat. fat), 0 mg chol., 7 mg sodium, 26 g carbo., 2 g fiber, 1 g pro. Daily value: 58% vit. C.

lemon crumb bars

Three convenient products—a cake mix, ReaLemon and Eagle Brand Sweetened Condensed Milk—team up to create made-from-scratch flavors (photo, pages 72–73).

Prep time: 10 minutes   **Bake time:** 15 to 20 minutes + 25 minutes
Makes: 24 to 36 bars

1	**(18¼-ounce) package lemon *or* yellow cake mix**
½	**cup (1 stick) butter, softened**
1	**egg plus 3 egg yolks**
2	**cups finely crushed saltine crackers (4 ounces)**
1	**(14-ounce) can Eagle® Brand Sweetened Condensed Milk (NOT evaporated milk)**
½	**cup ReaLemon® Lemon Juice from Concentrate**

Preheat oven to 350°. Beat cake mix, butter and 1 egg in large bowl with mixer until crumbly. Stir in saltine crumbs. Set aside 2 cups crumb mixture. Press remaining crumb mixture on bottom of greased 13x9-inch baking pan. Bake 15 to 20 minutes or until lightly golden.

Beat 3 egg yolks, Eagle Brand and ReaLemon with mixer or wire whisk. Spread over prepared crust. Top with reserved crumb mixture. Bake 25 minutes longer or until set and top is golden. Cool.

Refrigerate within 2 hours. Cut into bars. Store leftovers covered in refrigerator.

Nutrition facts per serving: 208 cal., 9 g total fat (4 g sat. fat), 51 mg chol., 256 mg sodium, 31 g carbo., 0 g fiber, 3 g pro.

blueberry citrus bars

We've added an elegant touch to the ever-popular lemon bar with a sprinkling of pecans and colorful blueberries (photo, pages 72–73).

Prep time: 10 minutes   **Bake time:** 20 minutes + 30 to 35 minutes
Makes: 24 to 36 bars

1	**cup (2 sticks) butter, softened**
¾	**cup sifted powdered sugar**
2¼	**cups unsifted flour**
½	**cup finely chopped pecans**
4	**eggs**
1½	**cups granulated sugar**
½	**cup ReaLemon® Lemon Juice from Concentrate**
1	**teaspoon baking powder**
1½	**cups fresh or thawed frozen blueberries**

Preheat oven to 350°. Beat butter in medium-sized bowl with mixer until fluffy. Add powdered sugar; beat until combined. Beat in 2 cups of the flour. Stir in ¼ cup of the pecans.

Press on bottom of greased 13x9-inch baking pan. Bake 20 minutes or until golden.

Meanwhile, for filling, combine eggs, granulated sugar, ReaLemon, baking powder and remaining ¼ cup flour in large bowl. Beat with mixer on medium speed 2 minutes.

Sprinkle berries over prepared crust. Top with filling and remaining ¼ cup pecans. Bake 30 to 35 minutes longer or until set and top is lightly golden. Cool.

Sift additional powdered sugar over top. Cut into bars. Store leftovers covered in refrigerator.

Nutrition facts per serving: 200 cal., 10 g total fat (5 g sat. fat), 56 mg chol., 105 mg sodium, 26 g carbo., 1 g fiber, 2 g pro.

*B*uttermilk Backup

No buttermilk in the fridge? Here's how to make a substitute: For each cup needed, place 1 tablespoon ReaLemon in a glass measuring cup. Add enough milk to make 1 cup total liquid; stir. Let stand for 5 minutes before using.

raspberry-lemon tart

Gorgeous, but so easy! This impressive dessert combines the tang of ReaLemon and the sweetness of raspberries for a sensational taste.

Prep time: 25 minutes **Bake time:** 12 to 13 minutes
Chill time: 4 to 24 hours **Makes:** 12 servings

½ **(15-ounce) package folded refrigerated unbaked piecrust (1 crust), at room temperature**
½ **cup granulated sugar**
¼ **cup cornstarch**
1¼ **cups water**
2 **eggs, lightly beaten**
2 **tablespoons margarine or butter**
½ **cup ReaLemon® Lemon Juice from Concentrate**
2 **cups fresh raspberries or sliced strawberries**
  Sifted powdered sugar

Preheat oven to 450°. Roll piecrust on floured surface to 11½-inch circle. Ease into 10-inch tart pan with removable bottom. Trim even with edge; prick well with fork.

Line with double thickness of foil. Bake 8 minutes. Remove foil. Bake 4 to 5 minutes longer or until golden. Cool.

Combine granulated sugar and cornstarch in medium-sized heavy saucepan. Stir in water. Cook and stir over medium-high heat until thickened and bubbly. Cook and stir 2 minutes longer. Remove from heat.

Gradually stir about half of the hot mixture into eggs; return egg mixture to saucepan. Cook and stir until almost boiling. Reduce heat; cook and stir 2 minutes longer. Remove from heat.

Stir in margarine or butter; gently stir in ReaLemon. Spread in prepared tart shell. Chill 4 to 24 hours.

Before serving, remove sides of pan. Place berries in center of tart and sprinkle with powdered sugar. Garnish with edible flowers if desired. Store leftovers covered in refrigerator.

Nutrition facts per serving: 166 cal., 8 g total fat (1 g sat. fat), 41 mg chol., 106 mg sodium, 22 g carbo., 1 g fiber, 2 g pro. Daily value: 12% vit. C.

Chocolate-Dipped Fruit

Cap off any dinner with an impressive, yet quick, dessert. Simply pour Eagle® Brand Creamy Chocolate Sweetened Condensed Milk into a pretty glass bowl. Then, serve it with whole strawberries and apple, pear or banana slices.

pumpkin-lemon bread

When it's your turn to bring treats to the office, surprise colleagues with this lemony take on traditional pumpkin bread.

Prep time: 15 minutes   **Bake time:** 50 to 60 minutes
Cool time: 15 minutes   **Makes:** 12 servings

1   **(14-ounce) package pumpkin quick bread mix**
2   **eggs**
½   **cup water**
⅓   **cup ReaLemon® Lemon Juice from Concentrate**
3   **tablespoons cooking oil**
⅓   **cup raisins**
1   **tablespoon sugar**
1   **tablespoon ReaLemon® Lemon Juice from Concentrate**

Preheat oven to 350°. Grease and flour 8x4-inch loaf pan; set aside.

Combine bread mix, eggs, water, ⅓ cup ReaLemon and oil in medium-sized bowl. Beat with wooden spoon until well mixed. Stir in raisins. Pour into prepared pan.

Bake 50 to 60 minutes or until toothpick inserted near center comes out clean.

Combine sugar and 1 tablespoon ReaLemon; brush over top of hot bread. Cool 15 minutes; remove from pan. Cool completely.

Nutrition facts per serving: 190 cal., 6 g total fat (1 g sat. fat), 36 mg chol., 203 mg sodium, 31 g carbo., 1 g fiber, 3 g pro.

creamy lemon pie

You'll taste a burst of lemon flavor in every bite of this rich and smooth pie.

Prep time: 10 minutes   **Bake time:** 30 to 35 minutes
Cool time: 1 hour   **Chill time:** 3 hours   **Makes:** 8 servings

3   **egg yolks**
1   **(14-ounce) can Eagle® Brand Sweetened Condensed Milk (NOT evaporated milk)**
½   **cup ReaLemon® Lemon Juice from Concentrate**
2   *or* **3 drops yellow food coloring, optional**
1   **(8-** *or* **9-inch) baked pastry shell** *or* **graham cracker crumb crust**
   Whipped topping *or* **whipped cream**

Preheat oven to 325°. Beat eggs yolks in medium-sized bowl with rotary beater or fork; gradually beat in Eagle Brand and ReaLemon. Stir in food coloring if desired. Pour into pastry shell or crumb crust.

Bake 30 to 35 minutes or until set. Remove from oven. Cool 1 hour. Chill at least 3 hours.

Before serving, spread whipped topping or whipped cream over pie. Store leftovers covered in refrigerator.

Nutrition facts per serving: 339 cal., 16 g total fat (6 g sat. fat), 97 mg chol., 137 mg sodium, 43 g carbo., 1 g fiber, 7 g pro. Daily value: 17% vit. A.

lemon chess pie

Bring a little Dixie charm to the table with this lemony version of chess pie, a longstanding Southern tradition.

Prep time: 15 minutes   **Bake time:** 10 minutes + 35 to 40 minutes
Makes: 8 servings

½ **(15-ounce) package folded refrigerated unbaked piecrust (1 crust), at room temperature**
3 **eggs**
1 **cup sugar**
2 **tablespoons yellow cornmeal**
⅓ **cup low-fat vanilla yogurt**
¼ **cup ReaLemon® Lemon Juice from Concentrate**
3 **tablespoons margarine *or* butter, melted and cooled**
1 **teaspoon vanilla**

Preheat oven to 450°. Press out fold lines and fit piecrust into 9-inch pie plate. Flute edge.

Line with double thickness of foil. Bake 5 minutes. Remove foil. Bake 5 minutes longer. Remove from oven. Reduce oven temperature to 350°.

Meanwhile, beat eggs in large bowl with mixer on high speed 5 minutes or until thick and light colored. Add sugar and cornmeal; mix well. Gradually stir in yogurt, ReaLemon, margarine or butter and vanilla. Pour into pastry shell.

Cover edge of pie with foil. Bake 25 minutes. Remove foil. Bake 10 to 15 minutes longer or until knife inserted near center comes out clean. Cool.

Store leftovers covered in refrigerator.

Nutrition facts per serving: 304 cal., 14 g total fat (2 g sat. fat), 88 mg chol., 187 mg sodium, 41 g carbo., 0 g fiber, 4 g pro.

Apples with Zing

If apples are overly sweet or mild, sprinkling them with a little ReaLemon or ReaLime before making a pie, crisp or sauce will ensure a great tart dessert.

key lime pie

This is it! The tart and cool classic that generations have enjoyed.

Prep time: 20 minutes   **Bake time:** 30 minutes + 15 minutes

Cool time: 1 hour   **Chill time:** 3 hours   **Makes:** 8 servings

- **3 eggs, separated**
- **1 (14-ounce) can Eagle® Brand Sweetened Condensed Milk (NOT evaporated milk)**
- **½ cup ReaLime® Lime Juice from Concentrate**
  Several drops green food coloring, optional
- **1 (9-inch) unbaked piecrust**
- **½ teaspoon cream of tartar**
- **⅓ cup sugar**

Preheat oven to 325°. Beat egg yolks in medium-sized bowl with mixer; gradually beat in Eagle Brand and ReaLime. Stir in food coloring if desired. Pour into piecrust. Bake 30 minutes. Meanwhile, for meringue, beat egg whites and cream of tartar with clean beaters to soft peaks. Gradually beat in sugar, 1 tablespoon at a time. Beat 4 minutes longer or until stiff, glossy peaks form and sugar is dissolved.

Remove pie from oven. Increase oven temperature to 350°. Immediately spread meringue over hot pie, carefully sealing to edge of crust. Bake 15 minutes. Cool 1 hour. Chill at least 3 hours. Garnish with strawberries if desired. Store leftovers covered in refrigerator.

Nutrition facts per serving: 364 cal., 15 g total fat (5 g sat. fat), 97 mg chol., 156 mg sodium, 50 g carbo., 0 g fiber, 8 g pro.

Lime-Papaya Sorbet

Lime-Mint Cake
(recipe, page 82)

lime-papaya sorbet

A simple sorbet goes gourmet thanks to the irresistible combination of papaya and a pleasing hint of ReaLime.

Prep time: 20 minutes   **Freeze time:** 3 to 4 hours + 6 hours
Stand time: 10 minutes   **Makes:** 8 servings

  2 **cups chopped, peeled and seeded papaya**
1 ¼ **cups sugar**
  1 **cup orange juice**
 ⅓ **cup ReaLime® Lime Juice from Concentrate**

Combine papaya, sugar, orange juice and ReaLime in large food processor bowl or blender container. Cover and process or blend until smooth. Transfer to 8x4-inch loaf pan. Freeze 3 to 4 hours or until almost firm.

Break into small chunks; transfer to chilled bowl. Beat with mixer until smooth but not melted. Return to pan; freeze at least 6 hours or until firm.

Before serving, let stand at room temperature 10 minutes. Garnish with fresh mint sprigs and edible flower petals if desired.

Nutrition facts per serving: 151 cal., 0 g total fat (0 g sat. fat), 0 mg chol., 3 mg sodium, 39 g carbo., 1 g fiber, 0 g pro. Daily value: 62% vit. C.

lime-mint cake

Just the right balance of ReaLime and mint enlivens this yummy dessert. It's perfect for showers or birthday parties (photo, page 81).

Prep time: 20 minutes
Cool time: 1 hour and 10 minutes

Bake time: 28 to 31 minutes
Makes: 12 servings

1   **(18¼-ounce) package white cake mix**
⅓   **cup ReaLime® Lime Juice from Concentrate**
2   **tablespoons chopped fresh mint**
     Lime Butter Frosting (recipe follows)

Preheat oven according to package directions. Grease and flour two 9x1½-inch round baking pans; set aside.

Prepare cake mix according to package directions, except substitute ⅓ cup ReaLime for ⅓ cup of the water. Gently stir chopped mint into batter. Pour into prepared pans.

Bake according to package directions. Cool in pans 10 minutes; remove from pans. Cool at least 1 hour.

To assemble, place 1 cake layer on serving plate; spread with about ¾ cup Lime Butter Frosting. Place remaining cake layer on top of frosted layer. Frost top and sides with remaining frosting.

Nutrition facts per serving: 487 cal., 15 g total fat (6 g sat. fat), 20 mg chol., 354 mg sodium, 87 g carbo., 1 g fiber, 3 g pro.

lime butter frosting

Beat ½ cup (1 stick) softened *butter* in large bowl with mixer until fluffy. Gradually beat in 3 cups sifted *powdered sugar* and ⅓ cup *ReaLime® Lime Juice from Concentrate* until smooth. Gradually beat in 3 to 3½ cups additional sifted *powdered sugar* until spreading consistency.

ake-Frosting Tips

For beautifully frosted cakes, begin with these simple hints:

■ **Before frosting the cake, brush off the loose crumbs with a pastry brush or your fingers.**

■ **To keep the plate clean, tuck strips of waxed paper under the edge of the cake.**

■ **Using a flexible spatula, spread the frosting with light back and forth strokes. Avoid lifting up the spatula so you don't pull the crust away from the cake.**

lemon-kissed cupcakes

It's amazing just how much flavor a dash of ReaLemon can bring to a simple cake mix.

Prep time: 15 minutes   **Bake time:** 15 to 20 minutes
Cool time: 5 minutes   **Makes:** 12 cupcakes

1   **(9-ounce) package yellow cake mix**
1   **egg**
⅓   **cup water**
¼   **cup ReaLemon® Lemon Juice from Concentrate**
2   **tablespoons sugar**

Preheat oven to 350°. Line 12 muffin tins with paper bake cups.

Combine cake mix, egg, about half of the water and 2 tablespoons of the ReaLemon in medium-sized bowl. Beat with mixer on medium speed 2 minutes. Add remaining water; beat 2 minutes longer.

Divide batter among prepared muffin tins. Bake 15 to 20 minutes or until toothpick inserted in centers comes out clean. Cool 5 minutes.

Meanwhile, combine sugar and remaining 2 tablespoons ReaLemon in small saucepan. Cook and stir until sugar is dissolved. Remove from heat.

Brush warm lemon mixture over tops of cupcakes. Cool completely.

Nutrition facts per serving: 99 cal., 2 g total fat (0 g sat. fat), 18 mg chol., 148 mg sodium, 19 g carbo., 0 g fiber, 1 g pro.

spiced lemon pudding cake

Try this luscious and lemony recipe when you want a dessert with an old-fashioned, heartwarming appeal.

Prep time: 15 minutes   **Bake time:** 35 minutes   **Makes:** 4 servings

½   **cup sugar**
3   **tablespoons unsifted flour**
¼   **teaspoon ground cinnamon**
¼   **cup ReaLemon® Lemon Juice from Concentrate**
2   **tablespoons margarine or butter, melted**
2   **egg yolks, lightly beaten**
1   **cup milk**
2   **egg whites**
   Sifted powdered sugar

Preheat oven to 350°. Combine sugar, flour and cinnamon in medium-sized bowl. Stir in ReaLemon and margarine

or butter. Combine egg yolks and milk in small bowl. Add to flour mixture; stir just until combined.

Beat egg whites with mixer to stiff peaks. Gently fold into batter. Transfer to 9-inch pie plate.

Bake 35 minutes or until top is golden and center shakes slightly. Sprinkle with powdered sugar. Serve warm.

Nutrition facts per serving: 245 cal., 10 g total fat (3 g sat. fat), 111 mg chol., 132 mg sodium, 35 g carbo., 0 g fiber, 6 g pro. Daily value: 26% vit. A.

best-ever
beverages

So, what's to drink? There's a colorful new twist on lemonade, for starters, and so much more, including pleasing punches, warming pick-me-ups and fruity slushes. Each clever concoction calls on ReaLemon or ReaLime to really make a splash.

Refreshing Berry Ade
(recipe, page 86)

Tropical Shake
with mango
(recipe, page 90)

Tropical Shake
with papaya
(recipe, page 90)

refreshing berry ade

This sipper is as pretty as a summer's day and the perfect complement to one, too (photo, pages 84–85).

Prep time: 15 minutes   **Stand time:** 20 minutes
Chill time: 3 hours   **Makes:** 8 servings

6½   **cups water**
2   **cups fresh *or* frozen**
     unsweetened raspberries
1   **cup sugar**
1   **cup ReaLemon® Lemon Juice**
     from Concentrate
     Ice cubes

Combine 3 cups of the water, 2 cups raspberries and sugar in large saucepan. Bring just to a boil, stirring to dissolve sugar. Remove from heat. Cover and let stand 20 minutes.

Press mixture through fine-mesh sieve; discard seeds. Transfer to pitcher. Stir in remaining 3½ cups water and ReaLemon. Chill at least 3 hours. Serve over ice cubes. Garnish with fresh raspberries if desired.

Nutrition facts per serving: 118 cal., 0 g total fat (0 g sat. fat), 0 mg chol., 12 mg sodium, 31 g carbo., 1 g fiber, 0 g pro. Daily value: 25% vit. C.

strawberry ade

Substitute strawberries for raspberries. Add 1 or 2 drops red food coloring if desired. Proceed as directed.

Nutrition facts per serving: 114 cal., 0 g total fat (0 g sat. fat), 0 mg chol., 13 mg sodium, 30 g carbo., 1 g fiber, 0 g pro. Daily value: 47% vit. C.

strawberry-citrus cooler

Looking for a nonalcoholic drink that's special enough for a party? Fizzy and festive, this concoction fits the bill.

Prep time: 10 minutes   **Makes:** 4 to 6 servings

3   **cups fresh *or* frozen**
     unsweetened strawberries
⅔   **cup orange juice, chilled**
½   **cup ReaLemon® Lemon**
     Juice from Concentrate,
     chilled
⅓   **cup sugar**
1   **cup ice cubes**
1   **cup lemon-lime carbonated**
     beverage, chilled

Combine strawberries, orange juice, ReaLemon and sugar in blender container; cover and blend until smooth. Slowly add ice cubes, blending until slushy.

Pour into pitcher. Slowly pour carbonated beverage down side of pitcher, stirring gently.

Nutrition facts per serving: 148 cal., 1 g total fat (0 g sat. fat), 0 mg chol., 15 mg sodium, 37 g carbo., 2 g fiber, 1 g pro. Daily value: 152% vit. C.

spicy mulled cider

ReaLemon adds just the right kick to this cool-weather favorite.

Prep time: 10 minutes   **Cook time:** 10 minutes   **Makes:** 8 to 10 servings

2 **quarts (8 cups) apple cider**
1 **cup firmly packed light
    brown sugar**
¾ **to 1 cup ReaLemon® Lemon
    Juice from Concentrate**
8 **whole cloves**
2 **cinnamon sticks**

Combine apple cider, brown sugar, ReaLemon, cloves and 2 cinnamon sticks in large saucepan. Bring to a boil. Reduce heat; simmer 10 minutes to blend flavors.

Remove spices. Ladle into cups. Garnish with apple slices and additional cinnamon sticks if desired.

Nutrition facts per serving: 212 cal., 0 g total fat (0 g sat. fat), 0 mg chol., 19 mg sodium, 57 g carbo., 0 g fiber, 0 g pro.

zippy tomato sipper

Call on this drink to add eye-opening appeal to your next brunch or lunch.

Prep time: 5 minutes   **Makes:** 4 servings

3 **cups vegetable juice, chilled**
¼ **cup ReaLemon® Lemon Juice
    from Concentrate**
1 **teaspoon Worcestershire
    sauce**
¼ **teaspoon bottled hot pepper
    sauce**
⅛ **teaspoon celery salt
    Ice cubes**

Combine vegetable juice, ReaLemon, Worcestershire sauce, pepper sauce and celery salt in pitcher.

Serve over ice cubes.

Nutrition facts per serving: 39 cal., 0 g total fat (0 g sat. fat), 0 mg chol., 729 mg sodium, 9 g carbo., 0 g fiber, 1 g pro. Daily values: 21% vit. A, 94% vit. C.

*L*iven Up Beverages

Accent tea, cola drinks, apple juice, fruit nectars or carbonated water with citrus zip by adding a few drops of ReaLemon or ReaLime. Or, freeze ReaLemon or ReaLime and water in ice cube trays to use in iced drinks without weakening their flavors.

spicy fruit cooler

Who says cinnamon and apple flavors are only fitting for fall? Spark the flavors with ReaLemon, serve over ice and you have a year-round refresher.

Prep time: 10 minutes   **Cook time:** 10 minutes
Chill time: 2 hours   **Makes:** 6 servings

¼   **cup water**
2   **tablespoons sugar**
2   **cinnamon sticks**
2   **cups apple juice, chilled**
2   **cups unsweetened pineapple juice, chilled**
2   **cups white grape juice, chilled**
½   **cup ReaLemon® Lemon Juice from Concentrate**
   Ice cubes

Combine water, sugar and cinnamon in small saucepan. Bring to a boil. Reduce heat; cover and simmer 10 minutes. Transfer syrup to small bowl. Cover and chill 2 hours.

Remove cinnamon. Combine syrup, apple juice, pineapple juice, grape juice and ReaLemon in pitcher. Serve over ice cubes. Garnish with fresh fruit if desired.

Nutrition facts per serving: 157 cal., 0 g total fat (0 g sat. fat), 0 mg chol., 10 mg sodium, 39 g carbo., 0 g fiber, 1 g pro. Daily value: 24% vit. C.

berry-pineapple slush

This fruity, lemon-sparked sipper is the perfect backyard beverage for warm days.

Prep time: 15 minutes   **Freeze time:** 24 hours
Stand time: 20 to 30 minutes   **Makes:** 8 to 10 servings

1   **(20-ounce) can pineapple chunks packed with juice, drained**
2   **cups fresh *or* frozen unsweetened raspberries *or* strawberries**
1   **cup orange juice**
¼   **cup ReaLemon® Lemon Juice from Concentrate**
2   **tablespoons sugar**
1   **(1-liter) bottle ginger ale, chilled**

Combine pineapple, berries, orange juice, ReaLemon and sugar in blender container or food processor bowl. Cover and blend or process until smooth.

Press mixture through fine-mesh sieve; discard seeds. Transfer to 2-quart square baking dish. Freeze at least 24 hours or until firm.

To serve, let stand at room temperature 20 to 30 minutes. Scrape across surface with large spoon and place slush in glasses. Add ginger ale; stir to mix. Garnish with fresh raspberries and mint sprigs if desired.

Nutrition facts per serving: 117 cal., 0 g total fat (0 g sat. fat), 0 mg chol., 15 mg sodium, 29 g carbo., 2 g fiber, 1 g pro. Daily value: 50% vit. C.

frozen daiquiri slush

Thanks to reliable ReaLemon and ReaLime, you can bring just the right balance of citrus flavor to this ever-popular refresher.

Prep time: 10 minutes   **Freeze time:** 6 hours   **Makes:** 6 to 8 servings

2 cups water
⅔ cup sugar
½ cup ReaLemon® Lemon Juice from Concentrate
½ cup ReaLime® Lime Juice from Concentrate
2 tablespoons rum, optional
1 (1-liter) bottle carbonated water, chilled

Combine water, sugar, ReaLemon, ReaLime and rum if desired in medium-sized bowl, stirring until sugar dissolves. Pour into 2-quart square baking dish. Freeze at least 6 hours or until firm.

To serve, scrape across surface with large spoon and place slush in glasses. Add carbonated water; stir to mix.

Nutrition facts per serving: 106 cal., 0 g total fat (0 g sat. fat), 0 mg chol., 44 mg sodium, 25 g carbo., 0 g fiber, 0 g pro. Daily value: 10% vit. C.

tropical shake

The combination of rich, smooth ice cream, tropical fruit flavors and a hint of zesty lime will take you straight to tropical paradise (photo, pages 84–85).

Prep time: 10 minutes   **Makes:** 3 servings

2 cups vanilla ice cream
1 mango *or* papaya, peeled, seeded and cut up
1 small banana, cut up
⅓ cup ReaLime® Lime Juice from Concentrate
1 cup ice cubes
¼ cup water

Combine ice cream, cut-up mango or papaya, banana and ReaLime in blender container; cover and blend until smooth.

Add ice cubes and water; cover and blend until frothy. Garnish with mango or papaya slices, toasted coconut and/or edible flowers if desired.

Nutrition facts per serving: 235 cal., 10 g total fat (6 g sat. fat), 39 mg chol., 77 mg sodium, 36 g carbo., 1 g fiber, 4 g pro. Daily values: 20% vit. A, 57% vit. C.

banana shake

This is no ordinary shake! Eagle Brand Sweetened Condensed Milk adds a velvety richness, making this drink extra luscious.

Prep time: 10 minutes   **Makes:** 5 servings

2 ripe bananas, cut up (2 cups)
1 (14-ounce) can Eagle® Brand Sweetened Condensed Milk (NOT evaporated milk)
1 cup cold water
⅓ cup ReaLemon® Lemon Juice from Concentrate
2 cups ice cubes

Combine bananas, Eagle Brand, water and ReaLemon in blender container; cover and blend until smooth.

Add ice cubes; cover and blend until smooth.

Nutrition facts per serving: 300 cal., 7 g total fat (4 g sat. fat), 27 mg chol., 106 mg sodium, 55 g carbo., 1 g fiber, 7 g pro. Daily value: 17% vit. C.

strawberry-banana shake

Reduce bananas to ½ cup. Add 1½ cups fresh *strawberries* or frozen unsweetened *strawberries* (thawed just until icy). Proceed as directed.

Nutrition facts per serving: 282 cal., 7 g total fat (4 g sat. fat), 27 mg chol., 106 mg sodium, 50 g carbo., 1 g fiber, 7 g pro. Daily value: 54% vit. C.

peach-banana shake

Reduce bananas to ½ cup. Add 1½ cups sliced, peeled fresh *peaches* or frozen unsweetened *peach slices* (thawed just until icy). Proceed as directed.

Nutrition facts per serving: 291 cal., 7 g total fat (4 g sat. fat), 27 mg chol., 106 mg sodium, 52 g carbo., 1 g fiber, 7 g pro. Daily values: 10% vit. A, 17% vit. C.

*L*emonade Sippers

Now you can enjoy the fresh taste of homemade lemonade without the work of making it from scratch.

■ Start with ReaLemonade™ Lemonade Liquid Concentrate and add water as directed on the package.

■ To make Lemonade Smoothies, combine 3 cups frozen unsweetened *peach slices* or whole *strawberries*, ½ cup ReaLemonade™ Lemonade Liquid Concentrate and ½ cup water in a blender container. Cover and blend until smooth. Immediately pour into 2 glasses.

cranberry-raspberry punch

No spring or summer celebration would be complete without this pretty pastel punch.

Prep time: 10 minutes   **Makes:** 12 servings

3 **cups cranberry-raspberry drink, chilled**
¾ **cup sugar**
¾ **cup ReaLemon® Lemon Juice from Concentrate**
1 **pint (2 cups) vanilla ice cream**
2 **cups sparkling water**

Combine cranberry-raspberry drink, sugar and ReaLemon in pitcher. Stir until sugar dissolves.

Pour into 6-ounce punch cups or glasses; add an ice-cream scoop to each cup or glass.

Slowly add sparkling water.

Nutrition facts per serving: 132 cal., 2 g total fat (1 g sat. fat), 10 mg chol., 32 mg sodium, 28 g carbo., 0 g fiber, 1 g pro. Daily value: 40% vit. C.

honey-citrus tea

Next time it's tea time, put something new in the brew with this sweet-tart pick-me-up. It's also great served over ice.

Prep time: 15 minutes   **Cook time:** 5 minutes   **Makes:** 4 servings

3	**cups water**
4	**tea bags**
1	**cup orange juice**
¼	**cup honey**
¼	**cup ReaLime® Lime Juice from Concentrate**
6	**whole allspice**

Bring water to a boil in large saucepan. Remove from heat. Add tea bags. Cover and let steep 5 minutes.

Remove tea bags. Stir in orange juice, honey, ReaLime and allspice.

Bring to a boil. Reduce heat; cover and simmer 5 minutes. Discard allspice. Serve hot.

Nutrition facts per serving: 96 cal., 0 g total fat (0 g sat. fat), 0 mg chol., 9 mg sodium, 25 g carbo., 1 g fiber, 0 g pro. Daily value: 36% vit. C.

lemon-lime iced tea

Iced tea never tasted so good. What's the secret? The dash of ReaLime adds an extra citrus spark.

Prep time: 10 minutes   **Cool time:** 2 hours   **Makes:** 4 or 5 servings

3½	**cups water**
4	**to 6 tea bags**
⅓	**cup ReaLemon® Lemon Juice from Concentrate**
¼	**cup sugar**
2	**tablespoons ReaLime® Lime Juice from Concentrate**
	Ice cubes

Bring water to a boil in large saucepan. Remove from heat. Add tea bags. Cover and let steep 5 minutes.

Remove tea bags. Add ReaLemon, sugar and ReaLime; stir until sugar dissolves. Transfer to pitcher.

Cool 2 hours. Serve over ice cubes.

Nutrition facts per serving: 54 cal., 0 g total fat (0 g sat. fat), 0 mg chol., 12 mg sodium, 14 g carbo., 0 g fiber, 0 g pro.

index

index

Metric Conversion Charts

Metric Cooking Hints

By making a few conversions, cooks in Australia, Canada, and the United Kingdom can use the recipes in this book with confidence. The charts on this page provide a guide for converting measurements from the U.S. customary system, which is used throughout this book, to the imperial and metric systems. There also is a conversion table for oven temperatures to accommodate the differences in oven calibrations.

Product Differences: Most of the ingredients called for in the recipes in this book are available in English-speaking countries. However, some are known by different names. Here are some common U.S. American ingredients and their possible counterparts:
- Sugar is granulated or castor sugar.
- Powdered sugar is icing sugar.
- All-purpose flour is plain household flour or white flour. When self-rising flour is used in place of all-purpose flour in a recipe that calls for leavening, omit the leavening agent (baking soda or baking powder) and salt.
- Light-colored corn syrup is golden syrup.
- Cornstarch is cornflour.
- Baking soda is bicarbonate of soda.
- Vanilla is vanilla essence.
- Green, red, or yellow sweet peppers are capsicums.
- Golden raisins are sultanas.

Volume and Weight: U.S. Americans traditionally use cup measures for liquid and solid ingredients. The chart, below, shows the approximate imperial and metric equivalents. If you are accustomed to weighing solid ingredients, the following approximate equivalents will help.
- 1 cup butter, castor sugar, or rice = 8 ounces = about 230 grams
- 1 cup flour = 4 ounces = about 115 grams
- 1 cup icing sugar = 5 ounces = about 140 grams

Spoon measures are used for smaller amounts of ingredients. Although the size of the tablespoon varies slightly in different countries, for practical purposes and for recipes in this book, a straight substitution is all that's necessary.

Measurements made using cups or spoons always should be level unless stated otherwise.

Equivalents: U.S. = Australia/U.K.

⅛ teaspoon = 1 ml
¼ teaspoon = 1.25 ml
½ teaspoon = 2.5 ml
1 teaspoon = 5 ml
1 tablespoon = 15 ml
1 fluid ounce = 30 ml
¼ cup = 60 ml
⅓ cup = 80 ml
½ cup = 120 ml
⅔ cup = 160 ml
¾ cup = 180 ml
1 cup = 240 ml
2 cups = 475 ml
1 quart = 1 liter
½ inch = 1.25 cm
1 inch = 2.5 cm

Baking Pan Sizes

American	Metric
8×1½-inch round baking pan	20×4-cm cake tin
9×1½-inch round baking pan	23×4-cm cake tin
11×7×1½-inch baking pan	28×18×4-cm baking tin
13×9×2-inch baking pan	32×23×5-cm baking tin
2-quart rectangular baking dish	28×18×4-cm baking tin
15×10×1-inch baking pan	38×25.5×2.5-cm baking tin (Swiss roll tin)
9-inch pie plate	22×4- or 23×4-cm pie plate
7- or 8-inch springform pan	18- or 20-cm springform or loose-bottom cake tin
9×5×3-inch loaf pan	23×13×8-cm or 2-pound narrow loaf tin or pâté tin
1½-quart casserole	1.5-liter casserole
2-quart casserole	2-liter casserole

Oven Temperature Equivalents

Fahrenheit Setting	Celsius Setting*	Gas Setting
300°F	150°C	Gas mark 2 (slow)
325°F	160°C	Gas mark 3 (moderately slow)
350°F	180°C	Gas mark 4 (moderate)
375°F	190°C	Gas mark 5 (moderately hot)
400°F	200°C	Gas mark 6 (hot)
425°F	220°C	Gas mark 7 (very hot)
Broil		Grill

*Electric and gas ovens may be calibrated using Celsius. However, for an electric oven, increase the Celsius setting 10 to 20 degrees when cooking above 160°C. For convection or forced-air ovens (gas or electric), lower the temperature setting 10°C when cooking at all heat levels.